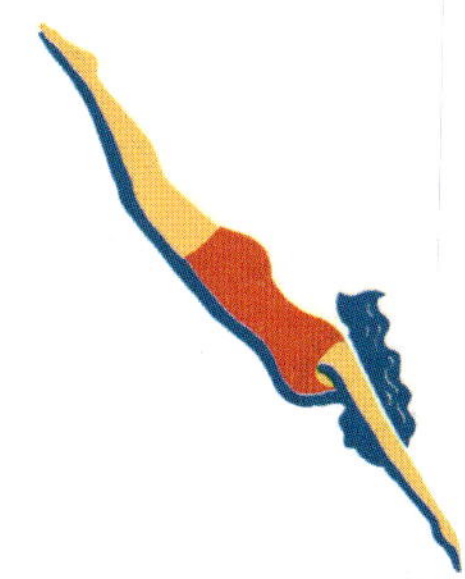

WILD SWIMMING
Walks

PEAK DISTRICT
28 lake, river & waterfall
days out

Matt Heason

WILD THINGS PUBLISHING

Walk 4, Slippery Stones

WILD swimming
Walks

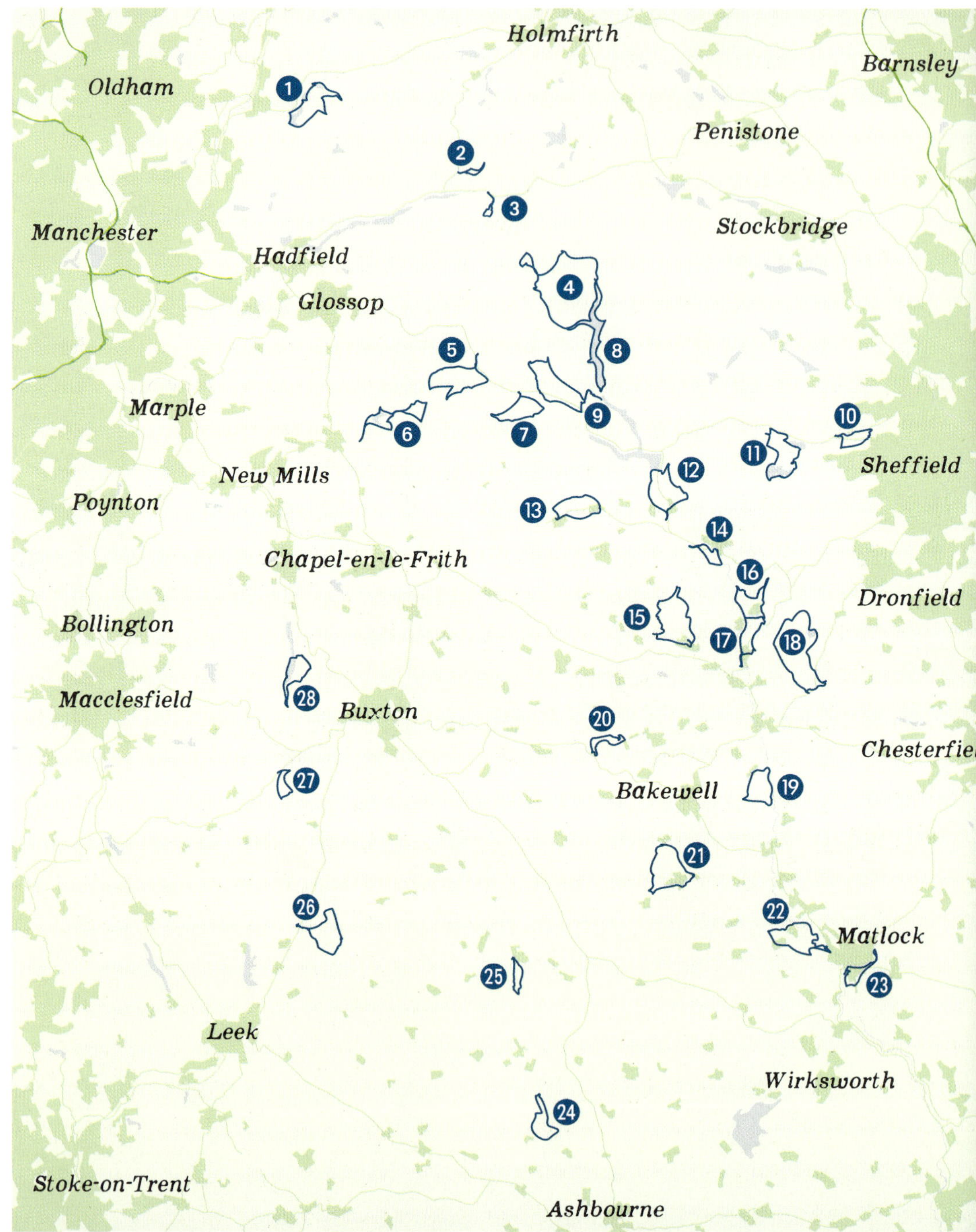

Holmfirth
Barnsley
Oldham
Penistone
Manchester
Stockbridge
Hadfield
Glossop
Marple
Sheffield
New Mills
Poynton
Chapel-en-le-Frith
Dronfield
Bollington
Macclesfield
Buxton
Chesterfield
Bakewell
Matlock
Leek
Wirksworth
Stoke-on-Trent
Ashbourne

THE WALKS

No.	NAME	SWIMMING
1	Dovestone Reservoir & Greenfield Waterfall	Pool at the top of the Greenfield Reservoir **S1**, then small pools in the river below the Trinnacle **S2**.
2	Withens Brook	Lots of pools, some up to chest deep in Withens Brook **S1 + S2**.
3	Black Cloughs	Countless pools and waterfalls on your way up **S1 + S2** and down **S3**.
4	Slippery Stones	Shallow Pools **S1**, a lovely pool in the upper reaches of the Derwent **S2**, before more isolated pools along the river **S3**, finishing at the amazing Slippery Stones plunge pool **S4**.
5	Fairbrook	Paddling early on in Lady Clough **S1**, with a good pool low on the upper Ashop **S2**, then lots of really good pools as you descend Fairbrook **S3**
6	Mermaid's Pool & Kinder Downfall	Beautiful plunge pools in the River Kinder **S1**, shower under the Kinder Downfall **S2** with a very shallow swim possible in Mermaid's Pool **S3**.
7	Blackden Brook Waterfall	Numerous plunge pools all the way up the Blackden Brook **S1 + S2**, with swimming also possible in the Ashop **S3**.
8	Dark Peak Two Reservoir Walk	Secret pool in Howden Clough **S0**, Slippery Stones **S1** pools and river **S2 - S4**.
9	Alport Castles	Possibility for a sneaky reservoir swim near the visitor centre, but 'it is not allowed'. A reedy dip in the lake underneath Alport Castle **S1**. Good dip and picnic spot by Alport Castles Farm **S2**, and below **S3** then multiple dipping spots along the Ashop River in the Snake Pass **S4 - S8**.
10	Rivelin Valley	Jump into and swim in the Rivelin Plunge Pool at the start/end of the walk just 100m from the car park **S1**. Other worthwhile spots along the River Rivelin including a low-angle slide **S2, S3 + S4**.
11	Redmires & Wyming Brook	Redmires Reservoirs **S1 + S2**, Rivelin Brook **S3**, Rivelin Reservoir **S4** and Wyming Brook **S5 + S6**.
12	Bamford Edge & Stepping Stones	Best spots are along the river bank just up-stream **S2** from the stepping stones at Bamford Mill **S1**.
13	Hope Valley	A series of lazy S bends in the river - **S1, S2 + S3**.
14	Hathersage Stepping Stones	Hathersage **S1**, N bank of Derwent **S2**, Stepping Stones **S3** and the bridge over the B6001 **S4**.
15	Waterfall Swallet & Bretton Clough	Waterfall Swallet **S1** & Stoke Ford **S2**.
16	Grindleford Derwent & Padley Gorge	Hay Wood shallow kids dip **S1**, Padley Gorge pools **S2 + S3** and then numerous spots on the River Derwent **S4 + S5**.
17	Froggatt Edge & Bridges	Waterfall on Froggatt Edge **S1** then lots of swim spots along the River Derwent **S2, S3, S5 + S6** with big jumping potential from the bridge **S4**.
18	White Edge	Silty swim at Ramsay **S1**, hidden pool by crossroads early in walk **S2**, then sublime moorland reservoir at Barbrook **S3** towards the end.
19	Chatsworth	Best between the two weirs **S1**.
20	Monsal Head	Lots of spots in the River Wye downstream from the viaduct **S1 + S2**.
21	Youlgreave & Lathkill Dale	Youlgreave Lido **S1** & the River Bradford **S2**.
22	Matlock Swoosh	Half an hour of floating down the River Derwent at the end of the walk **S1**.
23	Lumsdale Falls & Matlock	Below Lumsdale Falls is a waterfall **S2**, Lumsdale Falls **S3** & The River Derwent **S1**.
24	Dove Dale & Ilam Rock	Plenty of waist to chest-deep spots along the River Dove. The best are marked **S1 - S4**.
25	Pike Pool	Pike Pool **S1** then paddling spots downriver by the bridges at **S2 + S3**.
26	Blake Mere & Ramshaw Rocks	Amazing Blake Mere pool **S1** at the beginning and end of walk.
27	Three Shires Head	Lots of waterfalls with shallow pools **S1 + S2** in the stream above the main pools at Three Shires Head **S3**.
28	Packhorse Bridge & The Goyt Valley	Small reservoir by car park **S1**. Shallow pools for dipping in the River Goyt below the Packhorse Bridge **S2 + S3**. It is also possible to swim in Errwood Reservoir despite the usual No Swimming signs **S4**.

TERRAIN	REFRESHMENTS	KM	DIFFICULTY
Reservoir paths, steep waterfall scramble, open moorland paths, steep grassy descent.	None.	10	Hard
Open moorland path, gradual stream-bed descent.	None.	3.7	Moderate
Steep wooded scrambling up and down with short exposed open moorland section halfway.	None.	3.7	Hard
Long & exposed. Forest track leads to open moorland paths, some boggy, steep descent to landrover track then tarmac.	None.	16.4	Hard
Fun easy scrambling onto high moorland. Exposed and steep final climb, then exposed rocky path before scramble down river bed.	None.	10.5	Hard
Reservoir paths lead to open moorland and narrow path by waterfalls, then rocky scramble to plateau, rocky path past Downfall and steep grassy descent past Mermaid's Pool. Exposed.	Shops & Pubs at Hayfield (start & finish).	13	Hard
Fun, easy scrambling to high, exposed moorland before steeply descending past shooting cabin. Short section without paths.	None.	7.5	Hard
Easy, relatively flat alongside reservoir under trees.	Kiosk at Fairhome Visitor Centre (start & finish).	16	Moderate
Steep path through forest to flagstone path on exposed moorland before technical descent past Alport Castles, and easy path back, though with one more climb.	Kiosk at Fairhome Visitor Centre (start & finish).	15.5	Moderate
Well trodden footpaths in the trees with some steep climbs and descents on steps.	Cafe near the start and halfway around.	6	Moderate
Easy paths by reservoirs lead to rocky path over exposed moorland to well trodden track through the woods before rocky path and steps climbing back to car park.	Cafe on Soughley Lane near the start.	12	Moderate
Very steep tarmac track leads to exposed open moorland then rocky descent through woodland with return along disused railway track.	Pub and shop in Bamford near the end.	9	Moderate
Easy flat walking through grassy fields with small climb on return leg.	Pubs, cafes and shops at start, halfway and finish.	7	Easy
Easy flat walking through fields, mostly under trees.	Pubs, cafes and shops in Hathersage (start and finish)	5	Easy
Starts across fields before climbing into Bretton Clough with short steep sections, finishing over exposed open moorland.	Tea Rooms, pubs and shop in Eyam, pub half way around.	12.5	Moderate
Well trodden rocky path through woods with optional river scramble descent before flat, grassy fields return.	Shop & Pub at start and finish, ice cream van and cafe halfway around.	8.3	Moderate
Rocky but easy access bridleway along edges before steep rocky descent into woods and easy path alongside river. Final rocky climb through woods.	Pub near the start and finish, shop & cafe half way around.	8.4	Moderate
Open moorland paths throughout.	Occasionally a coffee van halfway round.	12.8	Moderate
Gravel vehicle track leads to open grassy path descent into estate grounds, then flat grassy walk alongside river.	Cafe at the start and finish.	6.7	Easy
Gradual descent on path through trees to river-side path, before steep climb up and over through woods.	Cafe & pub at Monsal Head (start and finish).	7	Easy
Mostly flat, easy paths and tracks with one short climb and descent.	Sometimes an ice cream van near the lido at Youlgreave towards the start.	10	Easy
Largely easy paths through fields and woods before long river swim.	Pubs at the end of the walk before the swim.	11	Easy
A mix of quiet tarmac roads and tracks, with some steep and narrow paths through woods.	Cafes & Pubs at the start and by Lumsdale Falls halfway round.	7.4	Moderate
Largely flat well-used riverside path, with one very steep climb through trees to open fields and a more gradual descent.	None.	8	Moderate
Flat grassy paths through fields to woodland and riverside path with foot bridges before climb on national cycle route back to Hartington.	Pubs and shops at Hartington (start & finish).	5	Easy
Descent from open and exposed moorland through farms and fields to climb through trees to Ramshaw, before difficult routefinding around edge of shooting range on return leg.	None.	8.7	Hard
Nicely graded descent on open moorland alongside river to pools before relatively steep return leg through quarries.	None.	5	Medium
Good quality paths and tracks throughout, beginning and ending on exposed high ground, with wooded middle section by river and reservoir.	Ice Cream van at Errwood Reservoir 3/4 of the way round.	8	Easy

Walk 26, Blake Mere & Ramshaw Rocks

INTRODUCTION

Walk 26, Blake Mere & Ramshaw Rocks

The Peak District, situated in the heart of England, is renowned for its breathtaking and distinctive scenery. The rolling hills, limestone valleys, woodlands and waterfalls tumbling from high moors and gritstone escarpments differentiate it from the surrounding industrialised and densely populated conurbations, offering a large area of peaceful, often tranquil, countryside which folk can freely visit. The Peak District is a national park, and the majority of visitors pass their time engaging in the popular and easily accessible pursuits of motoring, walking and cycling. This guidebook, however, offers an alternative approach and a more thrilling experience.

Wild swimming provides you with the opportunity to form an intimate connection with nature, an escape from the modern world and a chance to embrace the invigorating sensation of immersion in nature's embrace. This guide caters to both seasoned adventurers and novices eager to experience the wonders of wild swimming. It is a comprehensive description of 28 inspiring walks, each thoughtfully designed to showcase the best of the region's landscapes and hidden water-based gems. Whether you seek thrilling river swims, waterfall scrambles or tranquil pool retreats, we have carefully handpicked the best locations for wild swimming adventures, often off the beaten track, each combined with enjoyable walks and fascinating historical connections.

THE STRUCTURE OF THE GUIDEBOOK

Each walk is a circuit, beginning and ending at the same point, usually a car park or a lay-by large enough to offer parking space. Parking is a constant problem in the national park, so please park legally and courteously. Coordinates are provided for you to navigate to the start of each walk, along with a detailed map, clear directions, swimming and dipping spots and points of interest. Distance is measured in kilometres and metres. Each route includes estimated walking times, difficulty levels and amenities, allowing you to tailor your adventure to suit your needs. Please ensure you read each walk chapter fully before embarking on your adventure so you understand the context of the grading; some walks require a degree of navigational expertise, some feature technical scrambling. Straightforward walks are included, but, sadly, the Peak District does not feature any wild swimming spots with practical access for wheelchair users; we tried to seek out and include such spots, but we were advised to accept that it just isn't possible.

All walks are accompanied by photographs to help guide and inspire you. We also provide safety tips and guidelines for wild swimming, a comprehensive code of conduct and notes on wildlife and conservation, so you can enjoy this activity responsibly and sustainably.

Downloadable route information to print out or transfer to your smartphone can be found at wildthingspublishing.com/peakdistrict. Insert the last two words of each chapter introduction, with no spaces or capitals. For example, for Walk 1 go to wildthingspublishing.com/peakdistrict/oflife.

SAFETY & COMFORT

CHOOSING THE RIGHT GEAR

Walking and swimming are two physical activities that arguably require no specialist equipment or clothing. But there are a few items that you might want to consider, to make your outing safer and more comfortable.

Footwear is an important consideration. The most important requirement is the grip of the sole, especially on wet rock. A grippy tread combined with soft rubber can be found on a wide range of good shoes. Seek advice if you are not sure. Neoprene socks can add a degree of warmth.

A simple change of basic clothing, sealed in a waterproof bag, is comforting to change into following planned or unplanned dips. Snacks and a basic first-aid kit are essential on some of the more remote walks, where a slip and a fall can happen easily. For this reason, we recommend tackling these walks with at least one other person.

Take a map and compass on all of the walks – and know how to use them. While the maps in this guide show the route, they do not contain the level of detail of an Ordnance Survey (OS) map (details of the relevant map are provided at the beginning of each walk). We also highly recommend carrying a charged mobile phone with the required offline OS maps installed. Many of the walks are in remote locations with no signal, so do not wait until you are at the start of the walk to load your maps. While it is theoretically possible to complete each walk by simply following the written instructions in the book, bracken can make route finding difficult at the height of summer, even on well-used footpaths, hence the suggestion to have maps on your phone too.

You might consider a waterproof bag for carrying your kit, a small dry bag or plastic bag

for stowing wet swim clothes between stops and a bag for collecting other people's rubbish (plogging is a Scandinavian term for walking/running and collecting litter, which is, sadly, a common occurrence in the national park). Walking poles can also be useful, especially on some of the steeper ascents and descents.

Whether you wear a wetsuit or not is a personal choice. On many of the walks the water is surprisingly cold, flowing from one of the many reservoirs in the Peak District. Our personal choice is that the exhilaration of short dips and swims in cold water compared with the downside of carrying, donning and removing wetsuits outweighs the benefits of the extra warmth. That said, if you plan to spend prolonged periods in the water (such as on Walk 26 – Matlock Swoosh) or you simply prefer the extra comfort, then take a wetsuit and don't let anyone judge you for it!

Walk 26, Blake Mere & Ramshaw Rocks

Walk 5, Fairbrook

Walk 1, Dovestone Reservoir & Greenfield Waterfall

Walk 26, Blake Mere & Ramshaw Rocks

Walk 20, Monsal Head

TERRAIN AND WEATHER CONDITIONS

The Peak District is not as mountainous as Snowdonia or the Lake District, but the terrain should not be underestimated; it can be both rugged and remote. The underfoot geology is either coarse grey/brown gritstone or slick pale limestone, and both can be slippery when wet; the limestone is particularly treacherous. Many of the routes qualify as basic scrambles, and competence on such terrain and sure-footedness are essential.

Much of the Peak District lies in the eastern lee of the Pennines, so the eastern walks will often be drier than those to the west, as clouds dump their loads on the higher grounds of Kinder and Bleaklow. Weather forecast websites and phone apps are excellent and should be consulted both before and, if possible, during the walk, especially on the more remote routes on higher ground. Snow is not uncommon in April and May, and hail in July and August, while heavy rain can fall at any time of the year. Water levels are not only directly affected by the amount of rain falling locally but, equally importantly, by rain falling elsewhere on high ground over the same catchment area. If in doubt about whether to enter a watercourse or catchment feature susceptible to rising water levels – don't do it!

WATER SAFETY

There is a basic expectation that, if you are using this guide, you are able to swim. Cold water can reduce your swimming endurance, and it can quickly cause hypothermia. Don't enter without first establishing an exit point, particularly in flowing water. Enter the water gradually and allow your body to acclimatise.

Never jump or dive into water without first checking the depth and whether or not there are any obstructions. Even if you have jumped and dived at a particular spot before, always check as the underwater environment is in constant flux.

Swim in groups wherever possible, or if swimming alone let people know your movements and take special care.

If you are concerned about water quality, cover cuts or abrasions with waterproof plasters.

The photographs in the chapters will give an indication of the water levels when this book was researched. If there is more water than in the photographs – and you are in any doubt – don't enter the water. Never enter the water beneath a weir, even if it looks benign; strong undercurrents form underneath the surface and are responsible for drownings in the UK every year.

DISTANCES, TIMES & DEPTHS

Because the guidebook suggests you stop, often multiple times on each walk, it is impractical to estimate the time you will take when including these stops. The times given at the beginning of each walk, therefore, do not include stops, so you will need to factor these into your planning based on your group size, the weather and your need for a speedy march or a leisurely day out. Distances are in metres and kilometres and are estimated.

Walk 17. Froggatt Edge & Bridges

Walk 28. Packhorse Bridge & The Goyt Valley

Wild swimming in the Peak District is not the same as in Snowdonia or the Lake District. Aside from the Derwent, rivers and streams tend to be small, and there are surprisingly few natural lakes. Consequently, the swim spots described in the book are often dipping spots where you can immerse yourself in the water, but you won't always be able to swim any great distance. If you are considering jumping into the water, always check the depth first.

LOCAL WILD SWIMMING COMPANIES AND ORGANISATIONS

With the boom in wild swimming, particularly since the pandemic in 2020, a number of local companies and organisations have formed. In an effort to support independent start-ups and help the dissemination of good practice and etiquette – i.e., if you want to buy wild swimming kit and/or learn how to enjoy the sport under the guidance of an expert, use these local companies:

- **Peak Swims** – Suzie offers indoor-, outdoor- and wild swim experiences in the heart of the Peak District: **Peakswims.co.uk**
- **Wild Moose** – Rachel makes quality clothing and innovative gear for use in all weathers, designed for wild swimmers, paddlers, surfers and all aquatic adventurers: **Wild-moose.co.uk**
- **Wild Sole Sandals** – Using natural materials, Tom and Faye make their own sandals for wild swimming: **Wildsolesandals.com**
- **SOUP (Sheffield OUtdoor Plungers)** – a Facebook group for wild swimming in the Sheffield area with over 13,000 members: **Facebook.com/groups/181406392266654/?locale=en_GB**
- **Outdoor Swimming Society** – For all things to do with wild swimming; they also have a very active Facebook group: **Outdoorswimmingsociety.com** & **Facebook.com/groups/outdoorswimmingsociety**

Walk 5, Fairbrook

ACCESS, WILD SWIMMING ETIQUETTE & COUNTRYSIDE CODE

ACCESS – A BRIEF HISTORY

It is important to understand your access rights and to know why the Peak District is an important access hotbed and how things might look in the future.

The Peak District is one of the busiest national parks in the world, with over twenty million people living within an hour's drive. It has, consequently, played an important role in the issue of access.

In 1884 the first 'freedom to roam' bill was proposed in a campaign for public access to the countryside. It failed but paved the way for reform. The new century saw a growing appreciation of the outdoors and the benefits of physical exercise. More people started to seek escape from towns and cities, which led to a growing conflict with landowners. In 1931 the government recommended the establishment of a series of national parks, but again nothing changed. In 1932 the famous Kinder Mass Trespass took place, with hundreds of people clashing with gamekeepers as they sought access to Kinder Scout, the highest point in the Peak District. In 1945 Labour's post-war reconstruction further developed the concept of national parks, but it wasn't until 1951 that the Peak District became the UK's first.

COUNTRYSIDE RIGHTS OF WAY ACT

In 2000, the Countryside & Rights of Way Act (CRoW) gave us a partial right to roam over about 8% of England. In the Peak District we are fortunate that much of the upland areas featured in the walks lie on open access land (denoted on OS maps by a thick orange border). It is legally permissible to roam anywhere on land so delineated, and not restrict walking to designated paths.

RESERVOIR ACCESS

Parts of reservoirs can make fantastic and safe swim spots but current bylaws prohibit swimming in almost all active reservoirs. In theory, fines of up to £500 can be levied, although there have been no known cases. The prohibition is ironic given the very strong duties the Water Act 1973 inferred upon reservoir owners to provide a wide range of recreational opportunities. Recently there has been an increased drive in the campaigning for access: an annual Kinder Reservoir Mass Trespass being a local example. Many of the walks in this book pass reservoirs where swimming clearly takes place. While we can't, at this stage, encourage you to enter the water in these reservoirs, we hope and believe that in time access will be granted. During this transitional period, should you choose to enter the water, you may be approached by security personnel. They are generally polite but may tell you fear-mongering stories. Always be calm and polite. Read up on your position on the Sheffield SOUP Facebook page and be aware of the real risks of swimming in cold water, so that you can make informed choices for yourself.

RIVER & LAKE ACCESS

While reservoir access is considered difficult, river and lake access is sadly not always straightforward either. Angling clubs have riparian rights to many of the riverbanks in the Peak District, which gives them access to fish but does not give them sole rights to the water. The same 'rules' apply wherever you choose to swim: be calm and polite and read up on your rights to try to avoid confrontations.

For more detailed information regarding access and your right to swim in open water visit **Outdoorswimmingsociety.com/is-it-legal/**

FIRES

Much of the upland areas mentioned in this guidebook are blanket peat bogs, a carbon-rich soil formed over thousands of years which can be highly combustible, fuelling fires that can spread rapidly across vast areas. Once started, peat fires can smoulder underground for extended periods, reappearing and reigniting even after the visible flames have apparently been extinguished. The combination of dry vegetation and hot weather can create a perfect storm for fire outbreaks, putting vegetation, wildlife and nearby communities at risk.

A major concern is the use of disposable barbecues, which pose a particularly serious threat during extended dry seasons. Many visitors are attracted to the Peak District's scenic spots for leisurely picnics and BBQs, but the improper disposal of such BBQs can quickly lead to catastrophic fires. The high heat generated by disposable BBQs, especially when placed on dry grass or peat-rich ground, can spark uncontrollable fires that spread rapidly through the vulnerable vegetation. In just a matter of minutes, a seemingly harmless BBQ can escalate into a destructive inferno, endangering the delicate ecosystems and wildlife that call the Peak District home.

Fires are banned for much of the year in the Peak District, and there are campaigns to prevent local shops from selling disposable BBQs. If you see a fire or lit BBQ during dry spells, report it to the police immediately.

CONSERVATION & RESPECT FOR NATURE

We believe in the importance of preserving these natural wonders for future generations and encourage responsible practices with a wish to educate readers on the significance of conservation: respecting local ecosystems and promoting sustainable tourism. With an influx of visitors to the Peak District and many other parts of the UK, combined with a decline in public spending on education and awareness on how to behave in the countryside (less than £2,000 a year has been spent over the past decade in promoting the Countryside Code), we feel it is important to not assume that the details of such conduct are a given. Here's a summary of the Countryside Code:

Walk 4, Slippery Stones

Walk 4, Slippery Stones

Respect everyone:

- be considerate to those living in, working in and enjoying the countryside
- leave gates and property as you find them
- do not block access to gateways or driveways when parking
- be nice, say hello, share the space
- follow local signs and keep to marked paths unless wider access is available

Protect the environment:

- take your litter home – leave no trace of your visit
- do not light fires and only have BBQs where signs permit
- always keep dogs under control and in sight
- dog poo – bag it and bin it in any public waste bin or take it home
- care for nature – do not cause damage or disturbance

Enjoy the outdoors:

- check your route and local conditions
- plan your adventure – know what to expect and what you can do
- enjoy your visit, have fun, make a memory

TAKING CARE OF OUR WILD SWIMMING SPOTS

The post-pandemic surge in popularity of both the Peak District and wild swimming has been at least partially driven by social media. Phone cameras and filters mean enticing images of previously quiet spots can quickly gather momentum online, much to the chagrin of some fellow wild swimmers. It is a difficult equation to balance. While everybody is entitled to access the countryside, there should be an expectation that those doing so respect the Countryside Code. Many websites and social media groups and pages prefer that locations are not shared with images, allowing people to explore and discover places for themselves. This guidebook clearly contradicts that principle, but it is hoped

that the words on these pages carry the ability to educate and influence where a single influencer's image might not. Walk 18 – White Edge features a local example which has become a victim of its own popularity. Little Barbrook Reservoir can become very busy during extended hot spells in the summer, forcing the land managers to temporarily close it to allow it to recover. If all visitors adhered to and respected the Countryside Code, the impact would be significantly reduced. But it does raise another important issue which is only likely to worsen with time. Little Barbrook simply can't cope with unlimited numbers of visitors. If you arrive at the parking area and find that it's full, please consider going elsewhere. You are not entitled to park badly or dangerously and swell the numbers simply because that's where you decided to go. Consider the restaurant or cinema analogy: if you arrived at either to find they were full, what would you do? You'd go elsewhere.

Walk 16, Grindleford, Derwent & Padley Gorge

Walk 4, Slippery Stones

Walk 4, Slippery Stones

Walk 4, Slippery Stones

POO LIKE A PRO

Go before you go. The best option is not to need the toilet at all. It's not always possible but try to use the toilet before you head out.

Find a proper toilet. If you're caught short, local hospitality (after buying something) or public toilets are the next best option. We've detailed these for many of the walks where they exist.

Last resort? Bury it. With no other option – and only away from popular spots – bury your poo. Dig a hole 15cm deep and replace the earth afterwards. Remove toilet paper and sanitary products in a sturdy zip-lock bag – paper dug up by animals is never a good look.

FLORA & FAUNA

The flora of the Peak District is a rich tapestry of colours and textures. Heather-clad moors stretch as far as the eye can see, with their vibrant purples creating a breathtaking contrast against the rugged terrain. Delicate wild flowers dot the meadows in spring, while ancient woodlands offer a lush retreat in the summer. Keep an eye out for rare orchids and carnivorous sundew plants, which add a touch of intrigue to your aquatic escapades.

The fauna of the Peak District reveals itself in both subtle and striking ways. The skies are graced by the majestic flight of peregrine falcons and the cheerful song of skylarks, while secretive otters and water voles glide on and beneath the water's surface. Dragonflies dance along the reeds and, if you're lucky, you might glimpse the iridescent flash of a kingfisher darting by. The rivers and reservoirs host a variety of fish species, enhancing the allure of wild swimming with the promise of a glimpse of underwater life.

Of the species you may encounter, there are too many to list here. However, it is important to note a few to be aware of:

COWS

The Peak District is a rural area comprising many livestock farms. Cows feature on a number of the lowland walks and should be treated with caution and respect. Walk around them as quickly and quietly as possible. Turning side on to them can make you appear smaller and less of a threat. Walk diagonally away from/past them at a swift but steady pace. Some people recommend carrying a stick so you appear more imposing should the cattle approach you. If you have a dog, keep it on a lead which you can drop quickly if approached by cows. Most dogs will make their way safely away from the cows, who will be more interested in the dog than they are in you.

BRACKEN & TICKS

Bracken poses two issues for walkers. During the summer months it can grow above head height, obscuring not only the paths but walls, fences, gates and stiles, making navigation particularly tricky. We recommend downloading some offline OS maps to your phone to aid micro navigation when encountering bracken. Don't underestimate it during late July and August.

Bracken is where ticks live. Whenever you have walked through bracken, especially if you are bare-legged, make a quick visual check and brush off any of the tiny insects. When you get home, check your body thoroughly and remove any you find with a pair of tick tweezers. Increasingly, ticks are being found to carry Lyme disease, which, while not deadly, can be serious and debilitating. It can be treated with antibiotics if caught early, so if a tick bite develops a circular 'target' mark, seek medical advice. It is still very rare, but it's best to be on the safe side.

ENDANGERED SPECIES

A number of endangered species inhabit the Peak District. Water voles live on the Derwent, around Froggatt, Alport and Youlgrave, and otters are making a slow comeback in the region. The greater crested newt is common in the White Peak area, while adders are commonly sighted around White Edge, and the brown hare is found on the high moors of Kinder and Bleaklow. The white signal crayfish is in steep decline, threatened by the red-clawed American crayfish.

For a full list see **Peakdistrict.gov.uk/looking-after/biodiversity/action-for-wildlife/action-for-species**. If you see any of the above, please keep your distance, respect their habitats and report your sighting to the Derbyshire Wildlife Trust to aid in their monitoring and protection: **Derbyshirewildlifetrust.org.uk/wildlife/record-sighting**

INVASIVE SPECIES

The water bodies featured in this guidebook are delicate ecosystems, vulnerable to the threat of cross-contamination by invasive species. Human activities, including swimming, can inadvertently introduce non-native plants and animals, disrupting the delicate balance of aquatic life. Invasive species, such as signal crayfish and Himalayan balsam, can outcompete native inhabitants, causing irreversible ecological damage. It's crucial for wild swimmers to be vigilant by following guidelines to prevent unintentional transfer of invasive species, thereby helping preserve the natural integrity of these waters for future generations of both aquatic life and outdoor enthusiasts. These walks suggest swimming in multiple different locations, so the rules below are particularly important:

Check – Before leaving your swim spot, check your clothing, shoes and any kit for mud, plant material or aquatic animals. Remove anything you find and leave it at the site.

Clean – Clean your gear/kit thoroughly as soon as you can, paying attention to areas that are damp or hard to access. Use hot water if possible.

Dry – Dry everything for as long as you can before using elsewhere, as some invasive plants and animals can survive for more than two weeks in damp conditions. If you can't dry kit between swim sites, take spares with you.

Walk 6, Mermaid's Pool & Kinder Downfall

LOOKING FORWARD

Researching and writing this guidebook has been a voyage of discovery. Although I have lived and worked in the area for nearly 30 years, I have discovered many new swim spots, paths, woodlands and crags that I didn't know existed, and I am confident there are more of the same out there. I used an array of largely free tools to research and plan the walks: Google Maps and Strava, existing guides, and Facebook and Instagram groups and pages. I'd urge anybody with a sense of adventure to go looking for themselves. In particular, on open access land on higher ground there are countless brooks, cloughs and rivers; often 'Falls' are indicated on OS maps, which gives the game away. During the writing of this book, I was introduced to a local swimmer who has made it her goal to swim in every pool on Kinder, painstakingly exploring each and every stream and clough!

WHAT THE FUTURE HOLDS

As I alluded to in the chapter on access, I hope and believe that we are on the brink of a huge moment in history for wild swimming. There are so many compelling reasons why swimming should be not just allowed but actively encouraged across England and Wales, in line with the regulations in Scotland and much of the rest of Europe. This change is coming thanks to the activism of groups like SOUP and passionate individuals like Owen Hayman (founder of SOUP), Nick Hayes (The Book Of Trespass), Kate Rew (founder of The Outdoor Swimming Society) and dozens of others. I believe that in my lifetime Fairholmes Visitor Centre at Ladybower Reservoir should become a managed 'Base of Leisure' (a concept championed in France), accessible to the urban populations of Sheffield, Leeds and Manchester. Furthermore, local water authorities should embrace the concrete science linking well-being with cold-water swimming, recognising it as a restorative and freely available medicine in an increasingly busy and challenging world. Anglers should share 'their' rivers with bathers and kayakers, and our education ministers should once again revisit the importance of teaching our youngsters how to swim and to respect the countryside. If you'd like to read more about my thoughts on management of the Peak District, check out this Blog written in 2020: **heason.7thwave.io/cgi-bin/renderpost.py?postid=1216**

FURTHER READING:

- CRoW Act: **Gov.uk/right-of-way-open-access-land/use-your-right-to-roam**
- Right To Roam Campaign: **Righttoroam.org.uk**
- Outdoor Swimming Society 16 Reasons for Swimming Access In Reservoirs: **Outdoorswimmingsociety.com/sixteen-reasons-reservoirs**
- SOUP reservoir access notes: **Facebook.com/groups/181406392266654/announcements**
- *The Book Of Trespass*: **Uk.bookshop.org/p/books/the-book-of-trespass-crossing-the-lines-that-divide-us-nick-hayes/1844434?ean=9781526604729**

Walk 9, Alport Castles

Walk 27, Three Shires Head

Walk 4, Ladybower Reservoir

COLLECTIONS

WALKS TO DO WITH YOUNG KIDS

SCRAMBLES FOR THE ADVENTUROUS

PICNIC HAVENS

HISTORICAL JOURNEYS

DOVESTONE RESERVOIR & GREENFIELD WATERFALL

Hands-on scrambling up Greenfield Waterfall grants access to the Trinnacle, a gargoyle-esque rock formation high on the moors.

ovestone Reservoir lies at the convergence of the valleys of the Greenfield and Chew Brooks, above the village of Greenfield, on Saddleworth Moor. The reservoir is on the western edge of the Peak District National Park. It supplies drinking water to the surrounding area, keeps the local streams and rivers topped up during the summer and provides a picturesque setting for several walks. It is one of four reservoirs collectively known as Dovestones (the other three being Yeoman Hey, Greenfield and Chew). When Chew Reservoir was built in 1912, it was the highest in Britain at 488m. Dovestone Reservoir, the largest of the group, was completed in 1967. It is clear during the journey to the start of the walk that the area is different from much of the rest of the Peak District. Despite its proximity to Oldham and other satellite districts of Manchester, Dovestone Reservoir, with its altitude and topography, has an altogether more remote and wild feel.

The moors which feed the reservoirs are made of blanket peat bogs formed over millennia, by partly decomposed plants, including sphagnum moss. The peaty bogs lock in carbon dioxide thereby helping to fight climate change. Not so long ago the moors were barren and bare because of industrial pollution – it is estimated that at the height of the industrial era, up to three tons of soot fell on every square mile of Northern England each day. Now organisations like Moors For The Future are working hard to turn the black moors green again. You can read more and get involved at Moorsforthefuture.org.uk.

The walk begins and ends at a large pay & display car park below the Dovestone dam wall. There is a public loo here, the only one on the whole walk. This car park is around 1km from

INFORMATION

DISTANCE: 10km
TIME: 3–4 hours
MAP: OS Explorer OL1 The Peak District – Dark Peak Area
PARKING: Dovestone Reservoir pay & display car park (SE 013 034; 53.5276, -1.9811)
PUBLIC TRANSPORT: Buses from Oldham to Greenfield/Tunstead (84, 180, 184 & 350)
SWIMMING: Pool at the top of Greenfield Reservoir **S1**, small pool upstream **S2**, pool and spout below retaining wall **S3** and small pools in the river below the Trinnacle **S4**
PLACES OF INTEREST: Dovestone Reservoir, Greenfield Waterfall, the Trinnacle
REFRESHMENTS: None
VARIANTS: It is possible, once up on the top, to continue past the Charnel Stones to the Chew Reservoir to extend your loop

the village of Greenfield, if you are arriving by public transport. The walk begins by traversing the track along the top of the dam **1**. Look to your right and you will have an immediate idea of the scope of the route as it passes Dovestone, Yeoman Hey and Greenfield reservoirs before climbing steeply up Greenfield Brook to arrive at the edge of the plateau overlooking the waters. The edge is peppered with impressive rocky outcrops, including the amusingly named 'Trinnacle'.

The first section of the walk is flat, on a gravel access road, providing fairly easy access for wheelchair users. Access to the water in the reservoir is not allowed, but it is very close by and not fenced off. Picnicking and paddling by the reservoir shore are a common sight. The track continues to the second reservoir, Yeoman Hey, where we cross over the top of its dam wall. On the east side of the dam leave the track along a narrow footpath through the heather on the east bank of the reservoir. This delightful path winds its way to the base of the upper Greenfield Reservoir, past foxgloves and bilberries.

Back on the northwest side of Greenfield Reservoir we now follow another access track to its end. Neo-Gothic stonework tells of the Victorian fashions of the day, in the extensive channels, tanks and walls that manage the water in the three reservoirs. At the upper end of Greenfield Reservoir is a large pool created by a stone wall/small dam. The pool, which is deepest by the wall, provides your first permitted swim spot **S1**. From here the path follows Greenfield Brook upstream past more pools and waterfalls, the best of which are found after about 300m **S2**. Another 300m brings us to an unusual topographical site: Greenfield Brook is joined by a tributary also labelled Greenfield Brook.

At this confluence lies the last of the stonework, a retaining wall with a piped outflow, which creates a vigorous artificial waterfall with a rocky plunge pool beneath **S3**. The next section, although not long, provides the most excitement of the walk, as the path delves into the stream bed to scramble over the gritstone boulders, some the size of small vans, passing more waterfalls and miniature infinity pools **S4**, to arrive near the edge of the plateau.

An indistinct path breaks away from the brook **5**, on the right, to climb to relatively level ground on the edge. Follow the path to an outstanding viewpoint and the Trinnacle: an unmissable three-pointed pinnacle of rock projecting into space, overlooking the first half of the walk. If you're sure of foot, the Trinnacle is very climbable but take care in wet or windy conditions – it is precipitous! From the Trinnacle continue along the edge for about 900m, with fine views to your right, to an incongruous memorial to James Patterson, an MP who died in 1857 by the 'accidental discharge of a firearm'! Continue for another 600m to a rocky outcrop with a plaque commemorating two local climbers who died while climbing in the Dolomites in 1972. This spot marks the point at which we leave the edge and descend, fairly steeply, for nearly 2km back to Dovestone Reservoir.

At the bottom of the descent is an attractive bridge and copse of trees on the left, which make a lovely final picnic stop. Immediately after the copse, on the right between the track and the reservoir, is a delightful memorial wood, each tree accompanied by a small plaque in memory of a loved one. The wood is well maintained, with benches in peaceful spots where you can sit and reflect while overlooking the reservoir before returning to your transport and to the maelstrom of life.

1 Initially head S, uphill out of the car park to the top of the dam, before turning L to head N along the dam. At the end of the dam wall turn R to follow the level gravel track along the NW shore of the reservoir, before continuing on a short section uphill to the dam below Yeoman Hey Reservoir. 1.7km

2 Cross the dam. Initially, bear R, then take the footpath on the L which follows the reservoir's E bank on a narrow path through the heather. Once past the reservoir, the path joins a track below Greenfield Reservoir Dam. Follow the track L (W) before turning R to arrive at the dam. 1.7km

3 Follow the gravel track along the N shore of Greenfield Reservoir for 600m to a large dammed pool in Greenfield Brook immediately before the stream reaches the reservoir **S1**.

4 Continue up Greenfield Brook, past another fine pool below a small but pretty waterfall **S2** after 300m. After a further 300m arrive at a third swim spot **S3** below an artificial waterfall, where Greenfield Brook splits. Continue up the R fork of Greenfield Brook, past many more waterfalls and shallow infinity pools, scrambling up the stream bed for 600m to a R turn away from the water.

5 Climb up away from the brook on a path that skirts the plateau overlooking the reservoirs. After 100m bear R. After a further

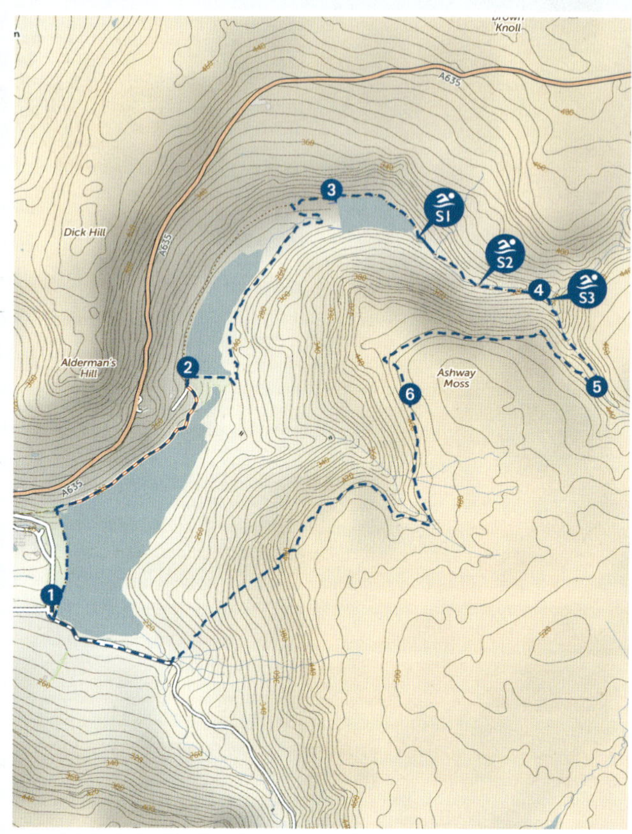

500m arrive at the impressive Trinnacle. Continue past the Trinnacle and bear L at a fork in the path after 400m. After a further 300m the path switches to a southerly direction. Keep to the edge of the plateau. Another 200m further on is a rather incongruous memorial cross.

6 After 600m turn L at a distinctive rocky formation with a plaque to Brian Toass and Tom

Mortion. Turn sharp L here and begin the steep descent back to Dovestone Reservoir. An attractive bridge is reached after 1.8km of descent. Cross the bridge and pass a small copse of trees as you approach the reservoir. The last leg of the walk is possible via the access road, or through a memorial wood on your R. The car park is 700m from the bridge.

Walk 2

WITHENS BROOK

Magical and far from the madding crowds, Withens Brook with its myriad pools offers great swimming and wading along its watery course.

In the Lake District they call it ghyll scrambling, and it's very popular in France and Spain, but it doesn't happen a great deal in the Peak District. The act of walking in a river is a much-underrated way to spend your time, and Withens Brook is the perfect place to give it a go. As this upland stream is narrow and shallow with no footpaths along its banks, it is easier to accept that your feet will get wet and wade into the water than it is to attempt to navigate the tussocks and bracken alongside. Of course, being reasonably steady on your feet is helpful, but the water is so clear that it's straightforward to navigate the rocky stream bed without undue problem. Dress with the expectation that you will very probably get wet, pack a dry bag for your essentials in case you do fall in, take some spare clothes and embrace being at the level of the lowly pond skimmers.

Begin by following the farm track from the lay-by, over a wooden stile, **1** through a gate and onto higher ground, for 1.7km to access Withens Brook. The route roughly follows the line of the brook, which lies down to your right. If you have plenty of time, push on further up to explore the upper reaches of the brook. We recommend arriving at the brook at an abandoned sheepfold. A short distance upstream from the piles of rock is a pleasant waterfall and pool **S1**, which marks the beginning of your descent. By now you will have experienced the tricky nature of the ground underfoot. At the pool change into your swimming gear, put on your shoes (any with a good grip will do, as long as you don't mind getting them wet) and jump in. Now ignore dry land and head downstream – in the stream. The rocky bed is largely gravel, small stones and flat gritstone slabs. You'll soon learn, hopefully, to recognise which are slippery and which aren't.

INFORMATION

DISTANCE: 3.7km
TIME: 1–2 hours
MAP: OS Explorer OL1 The Peak District – Dark Peak Area
PARKING: Small lay-by at the end of a farm track on the A6024 at Heyden Bridge. Park alongside the boulders without blocking the gate (SE 099 008; 53.5044, -1.8520)
PUBLIC TRANSPORT: None
SWIMMING: Lots of pools, some up to chest deep in Withens Brook **S1** + **S2**
PLACES OF INTEREST: Withens Brook Pools
REFRESHMENTS: None
VARIANTS: As this walk is relatively short, it can easily be done in conjunction with Walk 3 – Black Cloughs – which is very close by

And you'll soon begin to reach more pools **S2**; most are fairly shallow, but some are deep enough for a plunge, with maybe a shower or three under the many waterfalls.

There are plenty of grassy spots alongside, good for bucolic picnics and sunbathing. Hopefully, you'll have allowed enough time to appreciate being down low at water level. Just as walking or cycling offers a new perspective on familiar routes often overlooked when driving, following a water course offers a slower pace, revealing the minutiae of what may previously have remained unnoticed. If you visit during the height of summer, the bracken on the banks will more than likely tower above you, in places giving you the feeling of being in a sheer-sided canyon. The foliage-shrouded walls alter the ambient sound, amplifying the rushing of many cataracts while deadening distant road noise. Occasionally, you will quite possibly startle a grazing sheep or a dipper lazily going about its everyday life in the secluded environs of the stream. Glance sideways as you wade, and you will gaze into the concealed world beneath the bracken canopy.

Arrive at a rotting wooden fence which spans the brook and surmount it carefully. Eventually, a second fence marks the edge of open access land, so it's time to leave the water world and climb back up to the farm track you passed along earlier, returning to your vehicle. Although short in distance, this walk is rich in sensory stimulation, with ample opportunity to cool off on a hot day.

1 From the lay-by cross the stile next to the metal gate across the farm track. Follow the track alongside the stone wall through a second gate, after which the track steepens. Where it forks, keep R. The track soon becomes a path, which passes a wooden fingerpost to the L to arrive at a rocky knoll and wall.

2 Bear L along a low rocky ridge, initially on a narrow footpath, keeping to the R edge of the moor with Withens Brook down to your R. The path becomes less obvious, eventually disappearing into tussocks. Continue in the same direction to an abandoned and falling-down sheepfold by the brook after 700m.

3 About 100m upstream from the sheepfold is a pretty waterfall and plunge pool **S1**, which makes a good place to turn and follow the brook downstream.

4 Follow the stream for 1.5km to the second wooden fence crossing the water. This marks the edge of open access land. There are lots of pools, the best of which is after around 500m.

5 Follow the fence to the R and climb over the broken stone wall to arrive at a wooden gate. Go

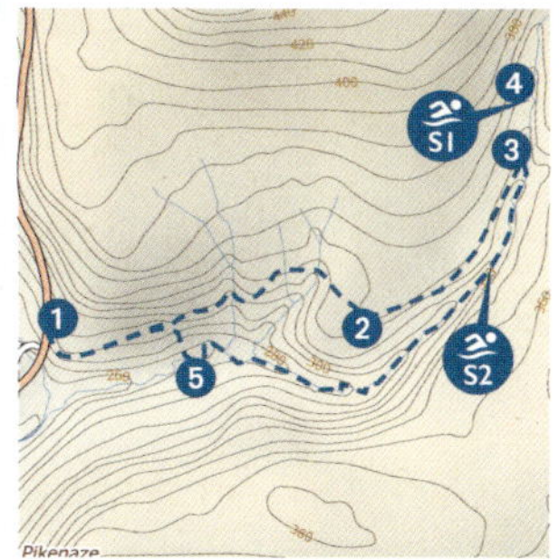

through the gate and follow a faint, diagonal path up the hill to the L to rejoin the track from where you started. Turn L on the track and return to your vehicle, 400m from the river.

BLACK CLOUGHS

A fantastic adventurous stream scramble up Near Black Clough, returning down Middle Black Clough.

This pair of gems, Middle and Near Black Cloughs, are pleasantly uncrowded and fall steeply from the delightfully named and very remote Featherbed Moss on Bleaklow to the Woodhead Pass: a busy east–west route between the cities of Sheffield and Manchester. Access to the lower pools is straightforward, but the walk itself is technical underfoot – steep and rocky – so we've kept the distance low to maximise the fun of stopping at the many pools and falls and to minimise the tricky walking in the upper reaches. Our route follows Near Black Clough upstream, before crossing to Middle Black Clough to return downstream. The two cloughs have another sibling, so if you have an adventurous bent, we'd encourage further exploration up Far Black Clough too. All three lie within a few hundred metres of each other, which results in a higher concentration of good pools here than anywhere else in the Peak District.

From the car park we are greeted warmly by the River Etherow as it immediately presents us with a series of beautiful pools ringed by wild flowers and picnic spots. A signpost by the car park instructs 'No Wild Camping' – always a good indicator of pretty places nearby! Cross the river on the bridge by the car park and immediately turn left to follow an access road alongside the pools **S1**. You'll probably want to tarry here but rest assured that there are plenty more to come. Continue along the track, which bends to the right. Shortly after the bend it fords a tributary making its way towards the Etherow; this is the combined flow of both Near Black and Middle Black Cloughs. If you fancy exploring Far Black Clough, ford the stream and follow the track which follows the clough for some distance. Our route does not ford the stream, but instead keeps right and ascends Near Black Clough.

From the large clearing, stay on the right bank, ignoring the obvious path behind you on the right, which does make its way to the upper reaches of Near Black Clough but at the expense of access to the water. Instead, keep close to the water and revel in the dozens of pools **S2** and falls as the path twists and turns and crosses and climbs. Around 1km after leaving the Etherow, the narrow, steep and twisting gorge opens out a little into a wider, more mellow valley lined with bilberries and heather. At this point the route bears left and climbs out of one watershed and crosses into the next. There are no paths along this 400m section, but you may be lucky and find a dry stream bed which allows easier progress to be made. Once out of the valley, look east for a collection of gritstone boulders that mark the upper reaches of Middle Black Clough. Head over the peat hags (patches of bare black peat) towards these rocks.

From the rocks begin your journey down the clough, past more pools and waterfalls. One pool **S3**, soon after you begin your descent, has a couple of stone slabs beneath the water arranged in the shape of an easy chair. Sitting in the 'chair' with the water around your neck, a fine spray from the waterfall plunging into the pool, is one of the highlights of the walk for some. A little further downstream a big slab of golden gritstone leans at a steep angle on the far bank of the clough, providing a fun gymnastic challenge: to jump the clough and land on the slab without falling into the shallow water.

Although the route along Near Black Clough is indistinct and you must forge your own path alongside the stream, the descent down Middle Black Clough has a very clear path if you keep to the right of the stream when following it downhill. Continue down, very steeply in places, past a large waterfall, to rejoin your route at the large clearing, crossing the water at this point to return the way you came.

1 From the large lay-by cross the bridge over the River Etherow below and turn L through the metal gate. Follow the track alongside the river, past the first pools **S1** offering swimming opportunities, for 500m before it bends R and forks at a ford.

2 Keep on the R side of the stream and follow it, ignoring the track that breaks R after 200m to continue upstream. Keep on the path on the R bank of the stream; it is narrow and steep and leaves the water and then returns. Follow for 1km until the gorge widens into a shallow valley.

3 At this point make a L turn, climb steeply up the heather- and bilberry-clad valley side. If you are lucky, you will find a dry stream bed to follow. If not, continue through the heather. Keep going across the peat hags on the top to a distinctive cluster of boulders (SK 116 983), which marks the upper reaches of Middle Black Clough. Head to these. The distance is 400m from clough to clough.

4 When you arrive at Middle Black Clough, turn L to follow the stream and path down past more pools **S3** and falls to arrive back at your outbound route after 800m.

5 Retrace your steps back to your vehicle. (800m)

SLIPPERY STONES

An adventurous and alternative route to the popular Slippery Stones via the Grinah Stones monsters.

This is a swim-walk of great contradictions. Ladybower, Derwent and Howden are reservoirs steeped in industrial history, yet remote and beautiful. Slippery Stones is a near-mythical plunge pool nestling at the head of the highest of the three reservoirs, far from civilisation yet surrounded by the cities of Northern England. Although the pool is only 15km from Sheffield as the crow flies, it will take you the best part of an hour and a half to drive to King's Tree, the memorial oak that marks the end of the tarmac at the upper reaches of the reservoirs, and then walk directly to the pool. This keeps the crowds at bay, but don't expect to have the pool to yourself. Such is its reputation that it is popular with walkers, cyclists and runners prepared to put in the effort to reach it. It is best to make a day of it and embrace the remoteness with a supremely scenic walk over the moors past the Grinah Stones. Get a good night's sleep, eat well and put on your walking shoes for an epic outing.

Construction of the neo-Gothic solid masonry Derwent Dam began in 1902, a year after the building of Howden Dam commenced, and proved a mammoth task. The chief engineer, Edward Sandeman, was awarded the Telford Medal in 1918 for his work. The huge stones that form the walls of the dam were transported along a specially created railway from the quarries at Bole Hill near Grindleford. Over 1,000 people lived in a self-contained town called Birchinlee or 'Tin Town', which was constructed for the workers. One of the metal huts was preserved and moved to the village of Hope, where it is now a hairdressing salon. Ladybower Dam was built between 1935 and 1943 to supplement the other two reservoirs in supplying the water needs of the East Midlands. It took a further two years to fill, which was completed

INFORMATION

DISTANCE: 16.4km

TIME: 5–6 hours

MAP: OS Explorer OL1 The Peak District – Dark Peak Area

PARKING: Ditch Clough Plantation, where the walk starts, is roughly 2km before King's Tree at the end of the road. If you have two vehicles drop your party here, continue to King's Tree, leave a vehicle there and return to your party, which will save you the 2km walk/hitch back along the tarmac at the end of the walk. Road open weekdays only (SK 155 927; 53.4311, -1.7674)

PUBLIC TRANSPORT: 272 bus from Hathersage to Fairholmes, which is 6.4 kilometres from the start of the walk. Bike hire available from Fairholmes

SWIMMING: Shallow pools **S1**, a lovely pool in the upper reaches of the Derwent **S2**, before more isolated pools along the river **S3**, finishing at the amazing Slippery Stones plunge pool **S4**

PLACES OF INTEREST: Grinah Stones; shooting cabins near point 6

REFRESHMENTS: None

VARIANTS: If you are short of time, you can park at King's Tree and head NW on a footpath up Linch Clough before connecting with Black Dike to join the described route at point 6

by 1945. Ladybower Reservoir is perhaps the best known of the three reservoirs, partly because it is remembered for the villages of Derwent and Ashopton that lie drowned beneath its waters. But it is also significant as the place where Guy Gibson and his men trained in their Lancaster bombers for the 'bouncing bomb' raid in 1943, destroying the strategically important dams of the Ruhr Valley in Germany, made famous by the 1955 epic film *The Dam Busters*.

Meandering your way along the banks of the reservoirs en route to King's Tree, you will see stone- and metal-work dating back to the construction years, with plenty of information boards and signage, to inform and educate, in the car parks and by the paths. It is very well done and maintained. Although the industrial heritage is evident everywhere, it is also a place of supreme beauty, with rolling grassy banks shelving to the water's edge, Canada geese, and sheep roaming freely beneath airy pine forests. The light in the valley is unlike anywhere else locally, bouncing and reflecting off the peaty waters and the green of the surrounding forests in an enchanting mix. It's hard not to be frustrated with Severn Trent Water, who manage these reservoirs, for not permitting any recreational access, although this does give the place a serenity that would be lost if shared with swimmers, sailors, canoeists and paddleboarders. Likewise, the dappled mossy forest floor would make for some truly outstanding camp areas, but it remains special and untouched.

The walk itself is yet another contradiction. While it delves far into the remoteness of the Eastern Moors it does so courtesy of a well-maintained network of forestry and grouse-shooting access tracks. We can only hope that, with time, hunting practices will diminish, but it will be important for walks like this to see some foot traffic to maintain the paths and single track.

Much of the walk follows easy tracks accessed by logging vehicles and rangers' 4x4s, although you are unlikely to encounter any. It begins very gently uphill alongside a picturesque stream with shallow pools flowing over gritstone slabs, a common sight in the area ❶ + ⑤. The lowland pine forest morphs into a smattering of ancient, gnarled oaks and birch stands, buzzing with giant dragonflies and grasshoppers, before the trees finally surrender to the upland specialists, bracken and heather. Do the walk in the middle of August, if you can, for a sea of purple akin to the lavender fields of southern France ❸.

A huge cooperative effort is underway to restore much of the high moorlands of the Peak District, which has suffered badly over more than a century of industrial exploitation and poor management. This walk doesn't delve too far into the worst affected areas, but where you encounter deep banks of bare black peat, do avoid walking on it; this is not its natural state and it can be quite boggy. The British Mountaineering Council, Eastern Moors Partnership and Moors for the Future, among others, are fundraising for teams of volunteers to plant sphagnum, a wonderful moss that binds the soil, reduces run-off and encourages the sequestering of carbon.

Once onto the moors proper, things flatten out before a faint track wends its way to the magical world of the Grinah Stones ❹. This chaotic collection of gritstone boulders has been shaped and carved by the elements, creating suggestions of huge stone monsters and faces. A favourite of local rock climbers, but so inaccessible compared with many other venues, it does not feature in any guidebooks and is left for each visitor to explore as

if pioneering. It's easy to spend a few hours scrambling, exploring and revelling in this hill-top troll fortress. If you have the time, and want more of the same, the nearby Barrow Stones add only an extra kilometre to the overall walk and provide a fine panoramic view north towards the Woodhead Pass.

When you've finished at the Stones, it's time to descend past two well-maintained shooting cabins **6** to the nearby source of the River Derwent **7** + **S1**, a young stream at this stage. Without any trees to shade their shallow waters, the pools in these upper reaches can be delightfully warm if they have caught the sun **S3**. Two or three kilometres of shallow, open flow over stone slabs means that

when the water arrives at your goal for the day, the amazing Slippery Stones **S4**, it's often unusually warm for a deep mountain pool. With a choice of ledges to jump from, the pool is around ten feet deep in the middle and a sheer delight to wallow in before continuing down the valley. You'll more than likely encounter others here, but there's room for a crowd. If you've timed it right and the sun is going down for your final few kilometres back to the car, this is where the play of light becomes magical.

All in all, it is a long but very fulfilling walk with some high-quality dipping and swimming spots, which make this one of the most rewarding walks in the Peak District.

1 Before starting be aware that at the height of summer the bracken grows very high and can make route finding fairly tricky. OS maps on your phone will be very handy if you have them. Park your car at the end of the long inlet 2km before King's Tree, by Ditch Clough Plantation. Alternatively, if you have two vehicles or a bike, leave your party here and continue to leave a car/bike at King's Tree, which means you can avoid the 2km walk/ hitch along the tarmac at the end of the day. Either way, park courteously and do not block the gateway. Leave the car and continue through the gate on a forestry track in a NW direction. Ignore the well-marked track that heads off steeply on the L after 200m. Continue along the forest track for 1.6km, passing potential shallow dipping spots on your R **S1**.

2 Where the forest opens out into more open land, cross the stream on a wooden bridge and continue through sporadic deciduous woods, climbing above the stream into the heather and bracken. The track passes through multiple wooden gates as it emerges from the trees. Follow two switchbacks before passing wooden grouse-shooting shelters as you head ever higher. (2.6km)

3 Many of the grouse butts (shelters) are numbered in descending order as you climb. At point 1 continue on level ground for a further 100m before turning 90 degrees L on a faint path across the moor in a NW direction. Continue past a large, shallow pond on your L (not suitable for swimming), for 600m, to take the L-hand fork. A further 400m brings you to a small stream, a fence and a wooden gate. This section can be quite boggy. Go through the gate and follow the track in a NW and then SW direction before it makes a beeline for the obvious Grinah Stones on the skyline of the hill above you. It is a steep climb to get to the stones, 1km in total. If you lose the path across the moor, don't worry, head for the obvious boulders on the skyline at the L end. It is open access land, so you are free to wander where you like, but the terrain is fairly difficult.

4 Picnic, rest and explore the maze of stones, before heading NE across the R edge of the plateau on top of the moor as far as a wooden gate in the fence on your R. Turn R and head downhill here. (900m)

5 From the gate head downhill for 400m to a stone cairn. Turn R in a SSW direction to arrive back at the track by which you originally crossed the moor to the Stones. Retrace your steps for 600m, past the pond, now on your R, to the forestry track **3**. (1.5km)

6 Turn L in a NE direction and begin to descend in an increasingly deep slot in the ground. After 500m in the peat-sided trench you emerge onto the side of a fledgling stream valley. Follow single track through the heather and bracken, past shooting cabins, for 2.1km, where a short, steep descent brings you to the River Derwent (very much a proper stream at this point), just a few kilometres from its source. (2.1km)

7 Head upstream for 100m or so to an idyllic waist-deep plunge pool with a gentle waterfall and overlooking birch tree for a well-earned dip **S2**. (100m)

8 Cross the stream on wobbly stepping stones and head steeply up through bracken and heather on a treacherous path, with ankle-twisting holes, to reach a 4x4 track on the opposite bank. (100m)

9 Follow the track SW and W for 3.3km, first on open moorland, then through broken oak and birch forest, down a pretty valley. Dipping spots can be found in the lower reaches **S3**. Eventually, you arrive at a wooden footbridge. (3.3km)

10 Before crossing the bridge, turn R and walk 200m NW towards the river to the main event – Slippery Stones **S4**. Once you've swum, retrace your steps to the bridge. Cross it and turn R, then take the R fork to cross a stone bridge over the stream. At 50m beyond the stone bridge there is a gate across the track. Go through this and follow the gravel road back through pine forest for a further 1.5km to arrive at King's Tree and the end of the tarmac road. (2km in total)

11 Depending on whether you were able to leave any transport here, either walk, drive, hitch or cycle for 2km along the tarmac road to where you left the car.

Walk 5

FAIRBROOK

Ascend to and then descend from the Kinder plateau via fairy pools and mossy picnic spots to search for crashed WW2 fighter planes on the high moorland.

Fairbrook is one of many small streams that fall steeply from the Kinder plateau to form gorgeous, bubbling amber-hued waterfalls and plunge pools en route. Thankfully, they are far enough off the beaten track to remain relatively quiet, but easily accessible for the sure of foot. The best approach is to descend Fairbrook Clough from the edge of the plateau north of Fairbrook Naze, a rocky outpost with panoramic views, but to do it from this direction requires an approach from the northwest via the remote-feeling Ashop Clough and Nether Red Brook. Interestingly, and tragically, on 22 July 1954 two North American Sabre fighter aircraft collided in the skies above this area of the Peak District. They were returning from an unsuccessful interception exercise to RAF Linton-on-Ouse near York when they either collided in cloud or flew into the western side of Kinder, scattering wreckage over a wide area of Ashop Moor; the remains of the two aircraft were not found for three days due to bad weather. We won't give you directions to the wreckage, but if you have time on your hands, we recommend the hunt!

This walk starts in a large lay-by on the north side of the A57 (Snake Pass), just up the road from what was the Snake Pass Inn. Cross the road and head down the zigzag path to Lady Clough ❶. Follow this on the east bank, after crossing a little wooden bridge on your left, ignoring the large bridge for logging vehicles on your right, and continuing through widely spaced groves of pine trees. Wild campers sometimes pitch their tents in this lovely spot next to shallow pools perfect for kids impatient to get into the water, but not deep enough for swimming ⑤①. About 700m

from the lay-by the Lady Clough river is joined by the River Ashop, a small stream which we will now follow. Cross the graceful wooden footbridge and turn right to follow the stream. The valley now opens out a little with a large dammed pool down to the left **S2** after a few hundred metres. This is a worthy first stop on your walk and is the best of the pools on the Ashop.

Continue upstream to another wooden gate. If you ignore the gate, the path follows close to the water, revealing more pools and small falls that require criss-crossing in places. For faster, more direct walking, go through the gate and skirt alongside, but some way above, the stream. The valley begins to widen out, with a high barricade of dark crags on the skyline to your left. Walk below this somewhat foreboding outlook, which evokes scenes from Lord of The Rings, when the fellowship are outrunning bands of Orcs through mountainous country! Approximately 2.5km from the footbridge, in the valley bottom, a small tributary enters Lady Clough from the left, having tumbled down through a steep ravine in the craggy skyline. This is Nether Red Brook **3**, marked by two distinct but low boulders in the heather either side of the watercourse. Take the faint path left and follow the brook up towards the ravine. Halfway up it is fenced off, but a stile high on the left allows access. Once over the stile make your way into the bed of the clough, by now usually completely dry, and scramble steeply up to the plateau.

Turn left **4** and follow the path along the rocky edge that you walked beneath earlier. After 1.3km you will arrive at a prominent outcrop of rocks called Fairbrook Naze. You will most likely want to stop here and take photographs, but be aware that it catches the wind horribly! Now follow the same path, which bends sharply to the right for a further

800m to the top of Fairbrook Clough **5** – your main objective of the day. Descend over boulders into the rocky bed of the clough, which is usually dry, then follow it down past dotted pools **6** to where two tributaries tumble from the plateau to initiate the flow of the stream. From here it gathers force and momentum, forming deep pools and waterfalls, many framed by ash and birch trees, creating some of the most photogenic swim spots on Kinder **S3**.

Stop as long as you can in the pools before descending back to the confluence with the Ashop. Don't cross the bridge here; instead, make a very short, steep climb on the left to follow a narrow path along the south bank for 1km **7** to the foot-bridge from where we commenced our walk. Cross this bridge, turn left and follow the Lady Clough back through the pine groves, over another foot-bridge and back to the lay-by **8**.

1 Cross the A57 to the footpath on the other side of the road. Descend into pine woods and bear L across a wooden footbridge on the E side of Lady Clough. Don't cross the large logging bridge, but instead follow the river through the trees past paddling spots **S1** to a graceful wooden footbridge where Ashop Clough joins Lady Clough. 700m in total.

2 Turn R to follow a path up Ashop Clough for 2.6km. The best swim spot is a picturesque dammed pool after 200–300m **S2**. The path passes by more pools as it follows and criss-crosses the clough, eventually opening out with Fairbrook Naze and Edge high in the distance on your L.

3 At 2.5km from the bridge, two boulders on your L (about 20m off the path) mark a faint path in the bilberry that leads up Nether Red Brook, at first a very small brook, which leads to a rocky cleft in the skyline. Follow the clough, keeping L at the fencing to cross a wooden stile, before rejoining the rocky clough bed to scramble to the top. 800m

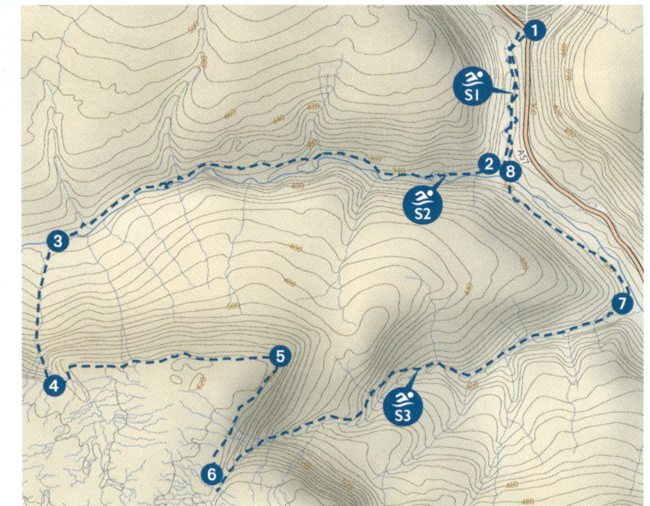

4 At the escarpment edge turn L and follow the rocky path for 1.3km to a prominent flat-topped boulder undercut on all sides (a great photo opportunity).

5 At the boulder turn R and keep close to the edge of the escarpment for a further 800m, at times following narrow ledges on the very edge; it is very exposed but has great views.

6 As the path nears the top of Fairbrook Clough, descend into the boulders which form the clough bed and drop down over rough ground to a better path that follows the watercourse as it grows and begins to form pools **S3**. 2.5km from top to bottom.

7 Once you arrive at the valley bottom, do not cross the bridge; instead, turn L to follow a faint path up the S bank of the Ashop for 1km, where an indistinct path leads R down to the river. Cross it on stepping stones to reach the bridge you originally crossed.

8 Recross the bridge and retrace your steps to your transport 800m away.

MERMAID'S POOL
& KINDER DOWNFALL

A walk steeped in the history of countryside access, it climbs the Kinder plateau to the Downfall, descending past the myth-laden Mermaid's Pool.

INFORMATION

DISTANCE: 13km
TIME: 4–5 hours
MAP: OS Explorer OL1 The Peak District – Dark Peak Area
PARKING: Bowden Bridge car park (SK 048 869; 53.3794, -1.9280)
PUBLIC TRANSPORT: 358 bus from New Mills
SWIMMING: Explore beautiful plunge pools in the River Kinder **S1**, shower under the Kinder Downfall **S2** and swim in the very shallow Mermaid's Pool **S3**
PLACES OF INTEREST: Kinder Downfall, Kinder Reservoir, Mermaid's Pool
REFRESHMENTS: Shops, pubs and cafés in Hayfield
VARIANTS: Can be combined with Walk 5 – Fairbrook – for a mammoth day out

On 24 April 1932 hundreds of men and women defied the law to walk over hills and moorland to the plateau of Kinder Scout in what would become the Peak District National Park. The protest was led by Benny Rothman, the twenty-year-old secretary of the British Workers' Sports Federation, which organised walks and cycling trips for young workers from Manchester and the surrounding mill towns. It followed a confrontation with gamekeepers, three weeks earlier, during an Easter camp when ramblers attempting to reach another peak, Bleaklow, were turned back. Six of the protestors were imprisoned, unleashing a massive wave of public sympathy that fuelled the Right to Roam cause. More recently, and more pertinently to a swim-walk guide, Kinder Reservoir has played host to well-publicised annual protest swims by those seeking fairer access to English and Welsh water bodies.

We begin the walk at Bowden Bridge National Trust car park **1**. Before leaving, take a look at the commemorative plaque, which details the original protest, on the quarry wall at the back of the picturesque parking area. The words engraved on the bench beneath provide much food for thought too, one of 50 installed in 2003 to celebrate the 50th anniversary of the formation of the Peak Park Ranger Service:

As i trudge through the peat at a pace so slow
There is time to remember the debt we owe
To the 'kinder trespass' and the rights they did seek
Allowing us freely to ramble the dark peak

The initial stage of the walk is rather tame, as it simply follows a tarmac road past a pretty campsite to the lower walls of the Kinder Reservoir dam. After just over a kilometre a gate in the wall **2** on

the left leads to a walled and paved path through rhododendrons to a vantage point on the west bank of the reservoir. Swimming in the reservoir is difficult to access, but clearly possible as evidenced by the protests.

The path follows the banks of the reservoir over a well-worn wooden footbridge to a second bridge ❸ over the River Kinder. At this stage in its genesis, it is little more than a babbling brook, but thanks to the precipitous nature of the terrain it has the wild swimmer's favourite tool to draw on: gravity. As our path winds its way up-river, criss-crossing the water on wobbly, moss-covered stones, small waterfalls have carved plunge pools of a satisfactory depth, making idyllic swim spots ❗ . We pass a picturesque plantation of mixed coniferous and deciduous trees, which attracts wild campers. The path deteriorates the further we venture, in keeping with the pervading air of wildness and historical significance.

As the path all but peters out, a small tributary joins the Kinder on our right ❹. From here it is possible to ascend to the Kinder plateau by either the Red Brook ❺ or the Kinder ❻. In winter they regularly freeze to provide moderate winter mountaineering routes. In summer they often dry

up, creating rare rock scrambles more common in Snowdonia or the Lake District. The gradient, while steep, is never dizzying, more of a collection of large gritstone boulders. For the best views of the Kinder Downfall, ascend Red Brook and turn left along the Pennine Way, which clings to the edge of the escarpment. For an even more challenging route to the top, continue up the Kinder itself, escaping to the left or right to avoid the cliffs at the top over which the Downfall pours S2 for most of the year. Both routes are challenging and require sureness of foot, good quality footwear and a head for heights.

When you have taken your fill of the majesty of the Downfall, continue along the Pennine Way for just over half a kilometre to some prominent rocks above a single-track path through the bilberry below to your left. Descend from the plateau to Mermaid's Pool S3. This site was thought to have been popular for ancient Celtic water worship rituals for a couple of reasons: firstly, unusually for an inland lake, the water is saline and, secondly, the water of Kinder Downfall often appears to flow upwards on a very windy day, giving it a mythical quality. The waters of the Mermaid's Pool are believed to offer healing qualities to those who bathe in them. The best time to visit is at midnight at Easter, the only time of the year when the mermaid is said to appear. If she looks upon you fondly, you will be granted the gift of immortality. Make sure you catch her on a good day, though, otherwise you can expect to be pulled into the pool to your death! Mermaids or not, the water is refreshing, but very shallow, with a peaty bottom.

The path down from the pool ❽ rejoins the River Kinder by dropping through the plantation of trees we passed earlier in the walk. From there it is a relatively quick trot back to the wooden footbridge ❾, followed by a few kilometres more to complete a circuit of the legendary reservoir ❿.

1 Park at Bowden Bridge car park. Leave the car park and follow the tarmac road NE for 1.1km to a footpath on the L, marked by a tall stone pillar and a wooden gate.

2 Go through the gate and follow the footpath around the edge of the reservoir for 2km, past its E most end, to a wooden bridge over the River Kinder.

3 Cross the bridge and turn L to follow the upper reaches of the River Kinder. The path is narrow, boggy in places, and criss-crosses the river on uneven stones. The best swim spots are around 800m from the bridge, just past a plantation of trees on your L, as the aspect steepens and waterfalls begin to form **S1**. After a further 400m the small tributary Red Brook joins the Kinder.

4 Turn R up Red Brook on discontinuous paths alongside the largely dry boulder-strewn course. Follow it with increasing difficulty, scrambling up the rocks, using hands where necessary, for 600m to reach the Kinder plateau.

5 Turn L to follow the rocky path (Pennine Way) along the rim for 1km to Kinder Downfall (**S2** if there is water flowing).

6 Turn L to follow the Pennine Way in a W direction for 600m to a L turn by some boulders. A narrow track can be seen in the bilberry scrub below the boulders.

7 Follow this path down to Mermaid's Pool, a small lake, after 600m **S3**.

8 Find the narrow path exiting from the SW corner of the pool and follow it to a plantation of trees. Pick a route through the trees to descend back to the Kinder river, close to the first plunge pools, and a short way upstream from the second narrow bridge.

9 Retrace your steps to the bridge (400m). Don't cross, turn L instead. After 600m a wall and gate mark the boundary of a private house. Bear L to skirt around this property, descending to stepping stones over a stream after 600m.

10 Continue over the stream to follow a path and track alongside a plantation on your R for 1km before arriving back at the tarmac road you started on. Turn L to return to the car park, a further 800m away.

BLACKDEN BROOK WATERFALL

Golden waterfalls and plunge pools abound as Blackden Brook tumbles from the Kinder plateau.

A word of warning: for this walk you will need to know how to use a compass and follow a bearing for around 400m across some open access land, which is covered in bracken for a period during the summer. The Kinder plateau is an extensive upland peat moor that attracts higher than average rainfall. The ensuing drainage takes the form of many streams of varying volume that run from the higher ground, cascading down the steep escarpments to form myriad waterfalls, rivulets, streams and pools. The gritstone bedrock imbues the peaty water with hues of amber and gold, absorbing the sun's heat and warming the shallow water far above the temperatures of the rivers in the valleys. Blackden is one such brook and there are many more, often running through open access land, so if you enjoy this one, go explore and find your own secret spots.

The route begins and ends on the Snake Pass, a feat of road construction under constant flux as the ground sinks and shifts. The resulting winding, hilly route is a favourite of both sightseers and thrill seekers, as well as forming an important commuter link between Sheffield and Manchester. It can be a joy to drive but is often busy with fast-moving, sometimes competitive traffic. Fortunately, much of the walk is confined within a steep-sided valley, so traffic noise is limited. Park in a large lay-by off the south side of the road. Take care pulling in and out as the kerb is viciously high. A wooden gate in the fence leads to a path which drops very steeply through a field to a bridge over the Ashop river ❶.

While there is the potential here to dip in the river by the bridge it is worth waiting, because not very far into the walk we arrive at the good stuff. Follow the path from the bridge up through a wooden gate and over a shoulder to arrive at Blackden Brook

INFORMATION

DISTANCE: 7.5km
TIME: 3–4 hours
MAP: OS Explorer OL1 The Peak District – Dark Peak Area
PARKING: Lay-by on the A57; free parking for 20+ vehicles (SK 130 895; 53.4021, -1.8058)
PUBLIC TRANSPORT: None
SWIMMING: Numerous plunge pools all the way up the Blackden Brook **S1** + **S2**, with swimming also possible in the Ashop **S3**
PLACES OF INTEREST: Blackden Brook, Kinder plateau
REFRESHMENTS: None
VARIANTS: From point 7 if you fancy another dip, there are a few pools in the lower reaches of Blackden Brook, accessible across the fields below the gate **S2**

after 600m. It is tempting to head straight from the gate down to the brook, but be patient and stick to the path, even though it feels as though it is heading away from the water. A few hundred metres after arriving at the brook is the jewel in the crown, literally a glimmering gem of a plunge pool deep enough to jump into – with care, it's four feet deep – below a frothing white fan of a waterfall, quite a magical picnic spot **S1**.

The path now follows the brook for around 1.5km, heading up and up. It is rocky and twisty, crossing the water several times, and not for the unadventurous. It has a very mountainous feel, akin to being in the Lake District or Snowdonia, and there is a multitude of pools deep enough to warrant a dip. About 1km after joining the Blackden is an impressive waterfall down to the left of the path, which climbs steeply along its right bank. There is, sadly, no plunge pool beneath this one, but it is, nevertheless, worth

picking your way carefully along the steep bank to the bottom of the fall to experience the thrill of standing beneath a significant fall of water and soaking up the misty energy.

Towards the top of the brook the ground becomes ever more broken, finishing in a jumble of boulders that have broken off the rim of the plateau. Either continue on the right up the Blackden or, a few hundred metres from the rim, follow a tributary to the left, which remains largely dry, for a fun but challenging scramble over car-sized chunks of gritstone **3**.

Once at the rim turn left to follow the narrow, single-file track for 2.4km, looking down on the narrow Blackden valley, and then continue onto the Snake Pass itself, the Ashop glinting at its base. The point at which we leave the plateau is marked by an obvious crossroads in the path **4**. Turn left to follow more single track as it bends around to the right, overlooking a linear series of grouse-shooting butts. These U-shaped stone shelters provide cover for hunters while they shoot at hapless, unsuspecting birds as they are flushed from the heather by beaters. A narrow, steep, grassy path takes a plumb line downhill past these butts before circling around to the right to an ugly, black-roofed, concrete shooting cabin (locked) **5**. From the cabin follow the steep access track to a sharp bend.

Don't follow the track down to the farm from the bend as there are no public footpaths back to the lay-by, and the reason is quite interesting! Downriver from the bridge at the start of our walk, visible from the hill as you are descending to the valley, is a curious arrangement of concrete and iron structures. The flow of the nearby Alport river, a tributary of the Ashop, is partially diverted by a weir to feed into the Ashop above an impound weir built in the 1920s to increase the catchment area of the Derwent Reservoir prior to the building of the Ladybower Reservoir downstream. The weir impounded the water and fed it into an open culvert (water conduit) that was built along the side of the hill. The culvert then feeds into a syphon over the river in a 6ft-diameter (1.8m) iron pipe before entering a tunnel to pass through the hill to the Derwent Reservoir via an open watercourse, entering the reservoir just north of the dam wall. The land around the workings is private, with no footpaths crossing it.

Instead of trespassing in the valley bottom, take advantage of the fact that you are on open access land and head in a WNW direction (bearing 290°) for 400m to arrive at a wall marking the boundary of the open access land. Follow the path along the left-hand side of the wall, back to the wooden gate **7**.

It will have been a while since you were last in or near any water, so if you need to cool down, from the gate head down to the Blackden and follow it upstream from the stone farm building for a few hundred metres to some small pools **S2**, before returning to the car via the bridge over the Ashop.

1 Park in a generous lay-by next to the A57, on the L as you are driving uphill (Sheffield to Glossop direction). Be aware that there is a high kerb to get into the lay-by, which is itself very rough. Leave the lay-by via the wooden gate and walk steeply downhill for 100m, through a field to the River Ashop. Cross the bridge then go through the wooden gate to climb steps and follow the path for 600m over a knoll to contour around to Blackden Brook. Don't be tempted to head straight down to the brook from the gate; be patient and keep to the footpath.

2 There are lots of swim spots over the next 1.5km as the path follows the brook, crossing from bank to bank, always rocky and technical and at times precipitous. The best spot arrives early, around 200m after you join the brook **S1**. Pass more spots as you continue up. Around 1km after joining the brook there is an impressive waterfall. It is accessible via a precipitous path down from the main path. No swimming, but worth a detour.

3 Continue past yet more pools, which become smaller as the flow dwindles. Around 200m before the top there is the option to turn L up a subsidiary stream bed to scramble up a jumble of giant boulders to the top. Advisable only for the adventurous and if the rocks are dry. Whichever route you choose to get to the top, you will arrive at a good footpath which follows the edge of the Kinder plateau. Turn L.

4 Follow the path along the edge for 2.4km to the first prominent crossroads in the single track. Turn L here.

5 The path begins to head downhill in a N direction before bending E. Continue to a grouse butte (small U-shaped stone shelter). Turn L at the shelter and follow a steep narrow path downhill along a line of similar shelters to a black-roofed shooting cabin (locked, and quite well hidden from above). Note that the cabin is visible from the top grouse buttes, but becomes invisible as you descend, eventually ending up on your L.

6 From the shooting cabin follow the access track downhill (NW) for 400m to where it bends R. Here strike off L onto the open access moorland on a bearing of 290 degrees (WNW). After 400m you will arrive at a wall marking the boundary between open access land and farm land. There is a good path along the wall on the uphill side. Follow this for 500m to arrive back at the gate through which you started. Much of this section can be covered in bracken for a period in the summer.

7 From the gate head back down to the Ashop where it is possible to cool off before **S2** heading back up the hill to the lay-by.

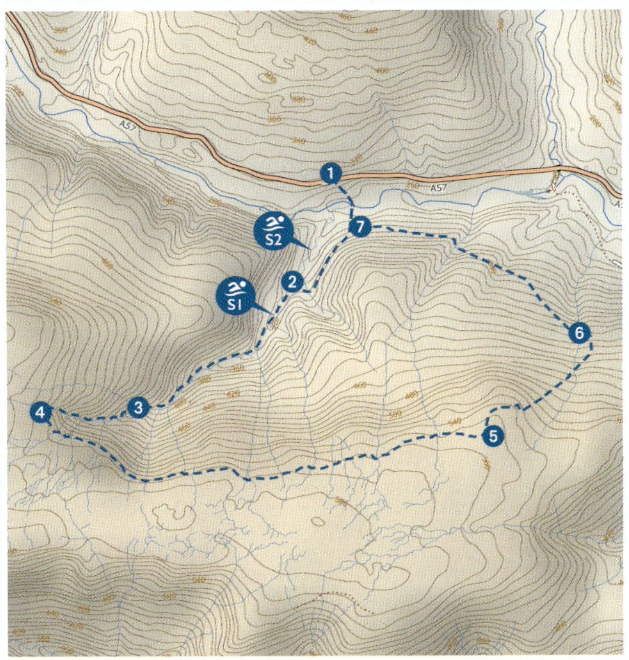

DARK PEAK TWO RESERVOIR WALK

A twist on the classic local reservoir circuit with some sublime secret swim spots overlooked by most.

It was tempting to think of this walk as 'easy' given its predominantly level nature and the fact that it is mostly on tarmac or forest track, but because it is a circular walk with no option to make it shorter, it is a step up from 'easy' due to its length. Having said that, it is one of the few swim-walks that is possible, and highly recommended, to do by bike. If you don't have your own bike(s), it is possible to hire them from the centre at the car park. Note that on Saturdays and Sundays the tarmac section on the west side of the reservoirs north of Fairholmes is closed to traffic, making cycling an even better option.

Don't let this summary lead you to the conclusion that this is a mundane walk. It is anything but. Steeped in history, it is a quite stunning mixture of dramatic open water views, seen up close thanks to the shore-hugging track, and lush forested glades, with some idyllic swim spots around the halfway mark. Let's address the elephant in the room, though. With a large dedicated car park and visitor centre to encourage visitors, and such proximity to the two reservoirs, why are we not recommending you swim in them? Quite simply, at the time of writing this book, swimming in Severn Trent's reservoirs is not allowed. Despite there being more open access in Scotland and much of Europe, local authorities persist with the misconceived notion that swimming is a dangerous activity, so rather than allowing it at the swimmer's own risk, they simply ban it. With luck, in the not too distant future, the campaign to have access to the likes of Derwent and Howden reservoirs, obvious natural resources, will be successful and this walk will become a classic, famous across the whole country.

The construction of the dams has been covered in Walks 5 (Fairbrook), 12 (Bamford Edge) and 16 (Padley), so instead we will talk about the history of the Dam Busters. Operation Chastise, commonly known as the Dambusters Raid, was an attack on German dams carried out on the night of 16/17 May 1943 by the RAF using special bouncing bombs. Before the Second World War, the Air Ministry had identified the industrialised Ruhr Valley, especially its dams, as important strategic targets. The dams provided hydroelectric power and pure water for steel-making, drinking water and the canal transport system. Calculations indicated that attacks with large bombs could be effective but required a degree of accuracy that RAF Bomber Command had been unable to attain when attacking a well-defended target. A one-off surprise attack might possibly have succeeded, but the RAF lacked a weapon suitable for the task. Without the accuracy to drop bombs vertically from altitude, and with German reservoir dams protected by heavy torpedo nets to prevent an explosive device from travelling through the water, the concept of skimming a bomb across the surface was practised. The dam on Derwent Reservoir was one of a handful used in practice ahead of the mission. The pictures of the breached Ruhr dams proved to be a propaganda victory and morale boost for the Allies while seriously hampering the Germans' progress. A popular film adaptation of the mission was released in 1955, parts of which were filmed on and around Derwent Reservoir. A memorial to the mission stands at the west end of the dam.

Our walk begins in the shadow of the mighty Derwent Dam. Walk north on the footpath from the snacks kiosk. If you visit during the summer, the chances are the water levels will be low, but in winter, water flowing over the top of the dam is a sight and sound to behold: a gigantic curtain of white water cascading over the resistant gritstone courses. Climb the steps at the east end of the dam to the level of the water behind it. Here we join a service track which follows the shore closely for its entire length. Note that if you are on bikes, this is the only deviation from the path you will need to make. Instead of carrying your bikes up the steps, head south, uphill, on a tarmac road to join the access track a few hundred metres downstream of the dam, before turning left to the dam.

The track is very easy to walk and affords fantastic views through the mixed woodland along the reservoir's shore. While much of the Peak District is bathed in yellows during the summer, the area around the dams is populated by purple rhododendrons and foxgloves, and the deep greens of spruce are peppered with copper beech canopies, all amplified by their reflections in the peaty water. Although 'No Swimming' signs abound, there is plentiful access to the water for most of the walk. Depending on the rainfall during the preceding months, there may or may not be substantial beaches between the water and the foliage. In particularly dry summers, when the water levels drop low enough, parts of old buildings appear, casualties of when the valley was flooded in the early 20th century. Follow the track for 3km to Howden Dam ❷. About 800m past Howden Dam is a stone bridge across Howden Clough. If you have time for an out-and-back excursion of around 500–600m each way, there is a deep, dammed-pool in the stream off to your right ❷, ⓢⓞ. Once back on the main track ❸ it is a further 2.7km to a meeting with another path and a narrow wooden footbridge ❹.

The swimming is concentrated north of the top end of the Howden Reservoir. Beyond its tip is the very young Derwent river, fresh from a spring only a few kilometres away on the high moors. Our route crosses a small tributary of the Derwent on a narrow wooden footbridge with a railing on only one side. If you are on bikes, it's fun to try to ride the ford upstream of the bridge. From here follow the narrow path to the left to a very special pool in the river **S1**. This is Slippery Stones, also featuring in Walk 4, which is approached from the moors to the west and north. Downriver from the pool are more, smaller pools **S2** which will very likely be less busy. Under the bridge is a lovely shallow pool **S3**, which warms nicely on a sunny day, and yet another a hundred metres downstream, where the wooden fence meets the water. Once you have picnicked and cooled off, head up the track from the bridge to a wooden gate. At 100m south of the gate a track on the left drops back down to a ford and some stepping stones over the river. It is worth an out-and-back trip to cross the ford and explore downstream in search of yet more shallow, pretty pools **S4**.

Back at the main track **6** continue for 1.2km, with open pine glades to your left and steep moorland to your right. Descend steeply to a concrete bridge before climbing back up to a gate at the end of the tarmac road from Fairholmes. In the middle of the turning circle at the end of the road is King's Tree, an oak planted in September 1945 by King George VI when he opened Ladybower Reservoir. Now follow the tarmac for 7.5km **7** as it winds its way along the banks of both reservoirs back to Fairholmes **5**. The spectacular views continue, especially in the evening as the light plays off the water. There is good access down to the water's edge for most of the route. Small sculptures commemorate Tin Town, the temporary settlements that housed the workers who built the dams. The walk finishes with a steep climb down from the top of Derwent Dam, ending in the car park at Fairholmes.

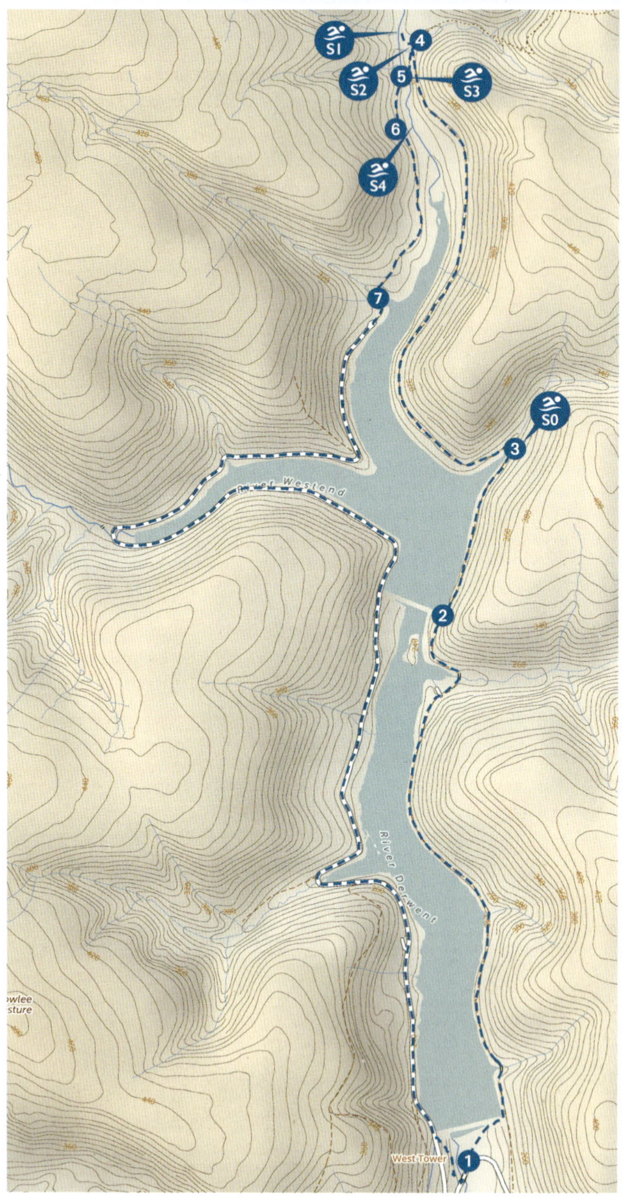

1 Park in the pay & display car park at Fairholmes. Follow the footpath N to the Derwent Dam. Walk underneath the dam, on the grassy meadow, to steps at its E end. Climb these to join a wide, flat gravel track that follows the bank of the Derwent Reservoir. Turn L to follow this track to the Howden Dam. (3.3km in total)

2 From the Howden Dam continue 800m on the gravel track. Before you cross a stream on main track there is a small path on the R-hand side up the side valley, Howden Clough. Follow this and slowly climb to the edge of the trees, around 450m. Exit the woods through a gate and proceed up the valley for another 150m, crossing the stream at the ford to arrive at a pool above a check dam **S0** (53.4387, -1.7337).

3 Retrace your steps to the main track and turn R onto it. Continue on the gravel track for a further 2.7km, passing through two gates, to arrive at T-junction by a wooden footbridge over a small stream.

4 Cross the wooden footbridge and turn L along a narrow path which leads to the River Derwent and a large, deep pool known as Slippery Stones **S1**, 200m from the footbridge. A further 100m downstream from Slippery Stones are a series of shallow pools **S2** which are usually less busy. There is more swimming in the large pool underneath the attractive stone bridge **S3**. Note that

Ordnance Survey maps identify the pool under the bridge as 'Slippery Stones', but locals will assure you that 'Slippery Stones' is the deep pool 200m upstream.

5 Cross the stone bridge and head uphill to a gate. Go through the gate to continue on the forestry track, heading S. Just 100m from the gate a track on your L leads down to the river. It is worth making a diversion down this track to the ford to explore the pools downstream **S4**. None are as deep as the first pool of the day, but they are lovely and peaceful.

6 From the T-junction off the main track continue for 1.2km to another gate and a roundabout with a tree in its centre – King's Tree.

7 From the tree, which marks the end of the driveable tarmac road from Fairholmes, follow the road for 7.5km back to the car park.

ALPORT CASTLES

A surprisingly straightforward walk through some very wild scenery featuring a high mountain lake amid geological chaos.

lport Dale is one of several wild valleys dropping from Bleaklow, an expansive upland moor close to the better-known Kinder plateau. While Kinder is criss-crossed with flagged footpaths and accessed from the popular villages of Edale and Hayfield, Bleaklow is a more remote and much wilder place. This circular walk skirts the edges of the higher ground, with panoramic views across the Snake Pass to Kinder in the west, and north-eastwards over the heather and peat hags of inhospitable Bleaklow. It can feel like you're swimming along the edge of an abyss: fascinated by what lies below but always able to gaze around from safe terrain and the reassuring security of a good pathway.

Alport Castles is a geological phenomenon, reputed to be the biggest landslip in the British Isles. It is a jumbled chaos of free-standing towers, fractured cliffs and boulder fields where, aeons ago, the edge of the plateau decided that Bleaklow was no place to be and made its way, catastrophically, down into Alport Dale and the Snake Pass. It sounds dramatic, and that's because it really is!

We begin the walk at Fairholmes Visitor Centre, where there are toilets, a snacks and drinks kiosk and a bike hire centre, handy for trips around Ladybower, Derwent and Howden reservoirs. Thankfully, just over the hill, Alport Dale was never dammed so that's where we're headed. While it may look enticing to swim in the reservoir by the visitor centre, it is owned and managed by Severn Trent and swimming is not permitted. The first opportunity to take a dip lies at the foot of the castle itself.

Follow the well-maintained footpath/track through magnificent beech woods **2** to Lockerbrook **3**, a bijoux outdoor education centre perched high above on a projecting shoulder of the moor.

INFORMATION

DISTANCE: 15.5km
TIME: 4–6 hours
MAP: OS Explorer OL1 The Peak District – Dark Peak Area
PARKING: Fairholmes car park (SK 172 893; 53.4005, -1.7422)
PUBLIC TRANSPORT: 272 bus from Hathersage to Fairholmes
SWIMMING: Possibility of a sneaky reservoir swim near the visitor centre – but it is not allowed. A reedy dip in the lake underneath Alport Castle **S1**; a good dip and picnic spot by Alport Castles Farm **S2** and below **S3**; then multiple dipping spots along the Ashop river in the Snake Pass **S4** – **S8**
PLACES OF INTEREST: Fairholmes Visitor Centre, Alport Castles
REFRESHMENTS: Fairholmes Visitor Centre has a snacks and drinks kiosk
VARIANTS: There is limited parking for a few cars where the route crosses the A57 near Alport Bridge. You could park here and simply walk down and back up the Ashop river if dipping and picnicking is your main objective. Alternatively, you could park where the route crosses the A57 at Hagg Farm, saving 3–4km walking up from and back down to Fairholmes at the start and finish, but parking is limited here. The section between the two road crossings along the River Ashop is very accessible with no hilly sections or rough ground

Once past the centre, look for a grassy track off to the right leading to a gate in the stone wall on the skyline. Here begins the really worthwhile stretch of the walk. For nearly 3km a footpath, sometimes flagged with great gritstone slabs, traces a line along the edge of the plateau **4**. Steep ground to the left hems the lower reaches of the Snake Pass. As the path gradually bends right, Alport Dale morphs from the lower reaches of the Snake below. Dotted with a handful of farmsteads, it's a reminder of what the valleys now submerged beneath the nearby reservoirs would have once been like.

The views to the left and right are very good, and after a couple of kilometres the crazy landscape of Alport Castles soon becomes the focus of attention. Although described as a landslip, it's hard to envisage how it was caused, or even what it might have looked like beforehand, or immediately afterwards. The description 'Castles' was probably chosen to describe the debris from the slide, which produced several tottering gritstone mounds that tower over the valley and appear from the distance to look like, er, castles. Viewed from

a distance the largest of these, the 'Tower', can be considered to resemble a motte and bailey castle. The rock faces and general jumblesome area are inherently unstable and no place for climbing and scrambling, unless the explorer has an affinity with A&E! However, paths criss-cross the boulder fields making them comparatively accessible, given their condition **5**. Ravens and peregrine falcons have been known to nest on the inaccessible cliffs. Below the western flanks of the Castles nestles a small but beautiful mountain lake, something of a rarity in the Peak District. While it's possible to take a dip here, it is very shallow (waist deep) and a bit reedy **S1**.

The remote Alport Castles Farm lies on the River Alport below the site; this is the farm where the suffragette Hannah Mitchell was born, in 1872, and brought up. Descend from the towers/lake on rough, steep ground through stands of rowan to the farm **6**. A very pleasant picnic and dipping spot can be found on the banks of the Alport, just upstream from the wooden footbridge **S2**. A hawthorn-lined farm track connects the remote farms in the valley to the Snake Pass **7**, and dipping spots lie down to the left of the track **S3**. Once across the busy A57, which links Sheffield and Manchester, cross the River Ashop via a weir or footbridge with a pleasant pool between the two **S4**. Follow the River Ashop, initially on its bank, past more pools **S5**, then tracks **8** and finally along a heather-lined terrace **9** into a shady pine forest. More spots **S6** – **S8** lie to your left but are not so easy to access.

The track back to Lockerbrook is steep and winding. It then retraces the route to the visitor centre **10**. While it would make sense to begin and end the walk at the lower of the A57 crossings, there is little parking here, and the road is infamous for speeding and accidents.

1 At 150m before the mini roundabout leading to the visitor centre, a footpath on the W side of the road heads W. Take this path into an airy beech wood. Continue uphill through the wood on a well-groomed track lined with trees, reminiscent of a French boulevard. Cross a working concrete aqueduct after 300m. Take the L fork after the bridge over the aqueduct signposted 'Lockerbrook'. Continue along single track through bracken for 200m uphill to a forest track. (500m in total)

2 At the forest track turn L. Follow a long R-hand bend for 200m to a wooden fingerpost and signpost. Turn L in the direction of Lockerbrook Farm. Follow a good track for 500m to a small gate. Go through the gate and continue for a further 200m to a T-junction with a farm track. (700m in total)

3 Follow the track L for 600m, past Lockerbrook, to a faint track trending back right up onto the moors. The grass track curves R to a gate in a stone wall on the skyline in 100m. Go through the gate and continue for 400m, gradually climbing to another wooden gate in a fence.

4 Follow the footpath with intermittent sections of flagstones for 2.8km, with views of the Snake Pass down to your L. Turn off the flagstones on a steep path down to your L towards the lower slopes of the Alport Castles.

5 Turn L and descend the path with Alport Castles on your R. After 100m it is possible, if you are sure of foot, and depending on how confident you are, to take a R turn and follow a very rough, rocky path around the back of the 'Castles'; this may add 10–20 minutes to your walk, but it is an adventurous and scenic alternative. It's even possible to leave this track on the SW side and scramble to the actual summit. If you stick with the main path, follow it for about 400m in a clockwise direction to a convergence of stone walls due S of the Castles. From here it's possible to take a faint path NW for 150m to the shallow lake below the Castles, maybe for a dip **S1**. Retrace your steps to the path.

6 Continue down steep and rocky terrain through rowan trees towards Alport Castle Farm. Stop at the footbridge over the stream. (750m)

7 Located 50m upstream from the bridge are picnic areas and pool access close to the path, but be aware you are within earshot of the farm **S2**, and undue noise would be insensitive. Once back at the bridge follow the footpath up to the R past the boundary of the farm through gates. Turn L on the farm access track and follow to the A57. Approximately halfway between the farm and the A57 are more pleasant stream-side picnic areas **S3**. Before the farm access track reaches the A57, turn L on a signposted footpath which leads to the busy road. (2.2km)

8 Cross the very busy A57, paying close attention to fast-moving traffic. Follow the tarmac track for 100m down to a weir over the River Ashop. Either cross the weir or use the footbridge upstream. Here are even more watery opportunities for aficionados **S4**. Now either follow the river E for a few hundred metres past good swim and picnic spots **S5** – and, rather randomly, an ancient football pitch on your R – before a climb up a steep, grassy bank delivers you to a 4x4 track, or follow the track itself. After 300–400m (depending on which route you chose), follow the track for 200–300m before turning off to the R just before it crosses the river (signposted 'Ladybower'). More picnic spots and dips are possible down to the L, although not all are as easily accessible as previous choices **S6**.

9 Follow the single track along a heather terrace high above the river. The final few places to access suitable water can be found after 400m, but some may consider these rather difficult to access, situated at the bottom of a steep bank **S7**. After a further 1.4km along a well-tended track, descend through a pine forest to a bridge over the River Ashop. More dipping spots can be found below the bridge **S8**.

10 Climb up the track to recross the often-hectic A57 and continue uphill on the access track to Hagg Farm before going through a gate on your R to climb up switchbacks to Lockerbrook Outdoor Centre after 1.7km. Retrace steps 2 and 1 to return to your car after a further 1.2km. (2.9km total)

S2
S1
5
6
7
S3
Rowlee
Pasture
River Derwent
West Tower
S5
8
3
A57
4
A57
S4
S6
S7
2
9
1
A57
10
S8

RIVELIN VALLEY

A magical short walk on the very edge of Sheffield, blending the city's industrial past with its proximity to the national park.

The Rivelin Valley boasted 28 water-powered mills in its heyday, the earliest dating back to 1580. They were used for many purposes: grinding corn, producing pulp for papermaking and manufacturing corset frames! Methodology on this esoteric craft is not readily available. It is apparent, during the latter half of the walk, where the mills used to be, an extensive network of goit channels, holding pools and dams still standing today. The first half of the walk contrasts with an increasing sensation of wildness as it climbs steeply through ancient deciduous woodland onto the top of Bell Hagg, a gritstone outcrop or 'edge'. The path hugs this edge with its unusually fine and expansive panoramas over Sheffield and what would once have been the busy mills.

As you leave the car park, you may hear the sound of laughter as youngsters play in the well-known Rivelin Plunge Pool **S3**, a generously sized natural pool with jumping potential from a height of about 3m. Although it is usually adequately deep enough, so there is no 'bottoming', it's always good practice to check this out before launching off. If a hot day is promised and you fancy a wake-up plunge to start things off, simply detour for 100m downriver to the pool before returning to the route after your dip **2**.

At the base of Blackbrook Woods is the Apple Shack **3**, a delightful shed in the back garden of a private house. Located right next to a verdant allotment in an open glade, it's rather sad that one comes across it so early in the walk. There again, it's fun to look at it as a compelling excuse to fuel up before the climb through the woods.

Sadly, the Black Brook is usually nothing more than a trickle with little cooling-off potential, but it does lead, via impressively

INFORMATION

DISTANCE: 6km
TIME: 2–3 hours
MAP: OS Explorer OL1 The Peak District – Dark Peak Area
PARKING: Public car park (free) on A57 (SK 290 872; 53.3811, -1.5642)
PUBLIC TRANSPORT: 257 bus from Sheffield Interchange, which is 9.7 kilometres away
SWIMMING: Jump into and swim in the Rivelin Plunge Pool at the start/end of the walk, just 100m from the car park **S1**. Other worthwhile spots along the River Rivelin, including a low-angle slide **S2** + **S3** + **S4**
PLACES OF INTEREST: Apple Shack Café, lido, heritage walk
REFRESHMENTS: The delightful family-run Apple Shack Café (drinks and home-made cakes) is open in the summer (also bell-tent glamping)
VARIANTS: When you have reached the edge, it is possible to drop off early or continue further on numerous side paths. The route back along the River Rivelin comprises many braided paths but works if you keep within sight of the river. 1.6 kilometres east (downstream) from the point at which you join the river **8** is Rivelin Paddling Pools, a lively open-air public lido popular with young families, but if you're visiting specifically, do check online whether it's open before turning up

Can also be combined with Walk 11 – Redmires & Wyming Brook

steep steps, to the edge of the Bell Hagg plateau **4**. Popular with climbers from Sheffield and the Peak District, the short but steep cliffs form a 1.5km intermittent barrier along the rim of the escarpment. The track at the base of the cliffs can provide entertaining views of rock climbers, but the cliff-top path is the better option, with excellent views over Sheffield.

The descent from the edge is notable because of two houses straight from the archives of *Grand Designs*, their choice of sites probably closely linked to the original ownership of the mills. Should you need a loo stop or perhaps another refreshment break, the Valley Side Garden Centre **6** can cater for both.

Once on the valley floor it's back towards the start **8**, following the River Rivelin past numerous industrial-age stonework and water-powered features. The area provides a rich haven for birds: we see herons, kingfishers, dippers, nuthatches and treecreepers. Just six miles from the centre of Sheffield, although the myriad trails are popular and easy to access, this haven offers adequate space to find peace and quiet and soak up the country atmosphere. It must once have been quite something: noisy, dusty and very smelly!

There are numerous dipping spots along the River Rivelin **S3** + **S4**, but most are less than waist deep. At a bend in the river a gently sloping bed is perfectly sited for sliding down on a rubber ring **S3**. The jewel in the crown hereabouts is the plunge pool **S1**, described at the start of this chapter **10**. On a weekday during school times you'll probably have it to yourself. On a hot summers weekend afternoon, you most certainly will not. Our experience, though, is of happy teenagers enjoying the outdoors, very little litter and a great atmosphere.

UPPER COPPICE WHEEL
The first mill was built in 1736 for
the Duke of Norfolk. By 1794 there
were nine grinding wheels for shaping
cutlery and razors. In 1854 Samuel Fox,
who started the Stocksbridge steelworks,
was making wire here. The outflow of
water from the nearby Rivelin Mill ran
to Coppice Wheel through a tunnel
which can still be seen upstream.

Rivelin Valley
Conservation Group

1 Walk out of the car park onto and across the road. There are various options but we suggest you keep the River Rivelin on your L, walking downriver. The Rivelin Plunge Pool **S1** is very close to the start and end of the walk, offering you the choice of whether to swim now, later or perhaps both! (200m)

2 Bear immediately R, away from the river, towards the A57. It is very busy so dogs on leads please, and shepherd youngsters. Once over the road turn immediately L for about 10m before bearing R to keep to the L edge of the private garden/drive. (200m)

3 Pass the Apple Shack, set back about 50m from the path on your R. Continue steeply uphill on either the L or R fork (both come out at the same place), with the Black Brook stream mostly hidden in dense vegetation on your L, for a further 400m.

4 At the top of the steep stone steps turn L to cross the Black Brook stream. This feels like you're following the edge of an escarpment, with a golf course on your R and steep, rocky ground falling away to your L. Impressive views of Sheffield extend on your L. (1km)

5 At a crossroads next to a striking architectural private house, keeping this modern cube house on your R, stay on the path, often overgrown and slippery when wet, as it drops steeply to the L. Continue to steep wooden steps down towards a main road and Valley Side Garden Centre. (0.6km)

6 Cross the busy A57 again and make a short dogleg to the R to a break in the wall. Descend steep steps past another striking house with huge windows. After 200m the path bends 90 degrees L before arriving at a gravel track. (400m)

7 Turn R and follow the track for 200m before bending back on yourself and beginning the return journey along the River Rivelin, crossing the ford at the green bridge. (200m)

8 Follow whichever path you choose but do keep as close as is practical to the river. The landscape is peppered with industrial remains, and there are numerous shallow pools in which to cool off **S2** + **S4**. After 700m there is a R-hand bend in the river which lends itself to sliding **S3**; it is especially good with a rubber ring.

9 Another kilometre of meandering footpaths along the river brings you to the famous local 12-foot plunge pool **S1**. Very popular on a hot day, as it is so close to the city, it is nonetheless charming. If you prefer, there are other quieter spots beforehand in which to cool off. (1km)

10 It's a short hop back to the car park, keeping the packhorse bridge on your L. (0.3km)

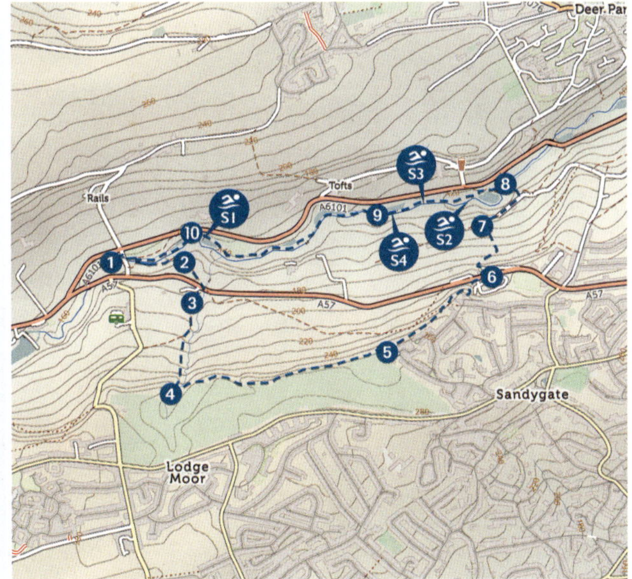

REDMIRES & WYMING BROOK

A wonderful walk on the edge of a major city with lots of potential to cool off, from open-water swimming in the reservoirs to dips and fun in the numerous pools and waterfalls of two beautiful brooks. Steeped in local history and a haven for wildlife and bird spotting.

INFORMATION

DISTANCE: 12km
TIME: 3–4 hours
MAP: OS Explorer OL1 The Peak District – Dark Peak Area
PARKING: Wyming Brook car park (free) (SK 268 858; 53.3687, -1.5974)
PUBLIC TRANSPORT: None
SWIMMING: Redmires Reservoirs **S1**, Rivelin Brook **S2**, Rivelin Reservoir **S3** and Wyming Brook **S4** + **S5** Swimming is prohibitied by bylaw in these reservoirs
PLACES OF INTEREST: Head Stone, Wyming Brook Shelter
REFRESHMENTS: Blue Moo Café on Soughley Lane at the beginning/end of the walk
VARIANTS: Follow the Long Causeway up to Stanage Pole. Head over the moors through the Rivelin Plantation instead of around the conduit track. Continue along the conduit track to the small reservoir at the end of the track for an adventurous swim

Can also be combined with Walk 10 – Rivelin Valley

Although it's possible to park on the roadside, we really recommend beginning and ending this walk in the car park, which has the benefit of being pleasantly shady. Begin by retracing your steps along Soughley Lane for 500m to the beginning of the public footpath. (If you're organised, it makes sense to drop any companions here on your way past, but please be considerate and don't obstruct the narrow road) **2**.

On the footpath your first swim spot is almost immediately as you arrive on the shore of the lower Redmires Reservoir. This is one of three reservoirs, a network of waterways and a surveying tower that were built between 1832 and 1854 following a deadly outbreak of cholera in nearby Sheffield, which killed 402 people. The reservoirs are still used to supply drinking water today, but the waterways have been superseded by pipework, providing havens for wildlife. Swimming is sadly still prohibited by bylaw.

There's a large patch of wild raspberries as you first arrive at the shore. At most reservoirs there are signs discouraging swimming, but people have been swimming here for years. The water is dark and peaty and warms up very nicely in hot weather, and there are several delightful picnic spots for 300m along the shore **S1**.

The path now leaves the waterside and ascends through heather and bilberry towards the middle reservoir. At the time of writing, this was undergoing repair work and was empty and cordoned off, but it is usually a popular spot for swimming. The path continues,

fairly close to the shore, then ascends to the level of the upper reservoir. Canada geese and squawking seagulls frequent the beach of the upper reservoir ❸. From here it is possible to extend the walk by heading up Long Causeway to Stanage Pole for great views towards the Peak District.

A short section of paved road runs along the shore of the upper reservoir ❹, past Redmires Plantation car park. The plantation is a gem of a spot, quiet and remote, and it is home to some very rare and endangered species. This Site of Special Scientific Interest (SSSI) is one of the few places locally where water voles can be found, and it also provides a haven for ground-nesting birds, such as the oystercatcher, the common sandpiper and the meadow pipit. We mention the plantation as it's possible here to deviate from our route description and strike due north from the plantation car park for a wilder walk over the moors before we rejoin the described route as it leaves the conduit track.

Redmires Conduit is a level track following ❺ a man-made water course which contours around the moorland fringe to a surveying tower, and beyond to a small reservoir. Now unused, the watercourse is an undisturbed home to a colony of water voles. Our route leaves the conduit track some way before the reservoir at a collection of gates **6** and heads north across the moors towards Rivelin Valley. Halfway down to the bottom of the hill is a crossroads of single-track paths marked by a short wooden fingerpost. Simply because it is so close, we recommend a quick there-and-back trip to the Head Stone **7**, an impressive, free-standing gritstone pinnacle that's visible from across the valley on the A57. The adventurous will climb the pinnacle – but note that the drop from the rear is particularly precipitous!

[Scan forward a few sentences to read about the best time to picnic at this spot]

Returning to the crossroads, we continue down the hill **8** through waist-high heather, a sea of bright purple during August, with opportunity to pick tart, purple-staining bilberries, eventually arriving at Rivelin Brook, a gorgeous stream laced with shallow, shady pools. Follow the brook **9** past many such pools **S3**. You may well choose to rest and picnic here, but there are better places ahead. *[The remainder of the walk will now be in the shade, so if it's a cooler day, you would be wiser to picnic earlier, by the Head Stone]*

Continue along the valley, climbing above the stream, past gnarly gritstone outcrops, contouring around the hillside, then descending to the lower Rivelin Reservoir **10** + **11**.

The reservoir is about 50m past where a footpath turns right up Wyming Brook for our return to the car park, but it is well worth the extra distance for a surprisingly private and undisturbed swim from a small beach **S4**. The water is shallow with a sandy bottom, usually pleasantly warm and quickly becomes deep enough for a proper swim.

The climb back up Wyming Brook **12** really is the jewel in the crown, a steep ascent past tumbling water glistening over mossy boulder steps, and

there are many, many pools **S5** to enjoy. None are swim spots, but all are beautiful. The path is comparatively popular because the car park is close by. Just before you arrive, there is an open glade of lush grass, stepping stones and stone dams creating shallow paddling pools, totally picturesque and a haven for families. For the adventurous who haven't had enough, the Wyming Brook Shelter is a little-visited natural cave beneath boulders; some have carvings dating back to 1944, reputedly inscribed by German prisoners of war who were billeted locally ★.

1 Exit the car park onto the road and turn L back along the road for 200m to a T-junction – be aware of traffic. Turn R at the T-junction onto Soughley Lane and continue for another 300m to a L-hand, R-angled bend. Some folk park here to access the reservoirs, but we suggest parking in the proper car park as described.

2 Turn R and head W on a wide gravel footpath signposted 'Public Footpath (Walkers Only)' for 100m to a wooden gate. Go through this and bear slightly L to join a footpath around the shore of the lower reservoir. There are access points to the water all along the shore for 300m. Officially, there is no swimming, but it is nevertheless a deservedly popular spot **S1**. Continue as the footpath climbs up and away from the water to join the level of the next reservoir. (1.1km)

3 Follow the footpath for 400m W before looping S and then back N to arrive at the end of a paved road by the bottom of Long Causeway. (800m)

4 Follow the paved road for 1km past Redmires Plantation car park.

5 After 400m from the car park, at the end of the reservoir, turn L at a public footpath sign by two metal gates to follow a conduit for 1.4km first N and then NW. When you get to a four-bar metal gate (with a stile on its R), turn R over the other stile, which is on the L of a six-bar metal gate. Follow the track downhill to a wooden stile. Cross this to continue N.

6 Walk downhill (N) on a narrow single track descending through heather for 500m to a crossroads with a small wooden fingerpost.

7 Turn L (W) for 300m to a prominent 4m-high gritstone pinnacle called Head Stone. Retrace your steps to the crossroads and fingerpost. (600m total)

8 Turn L to head N and continue descending through heather and bracken to reach Rivelin Brook. (300m)

9 Cross the bridge and turn R to head E and follow Rivelin Brook on its N bank, passing small but shallow pools which could be perfect for a cooling-off intermission **S2**. At 600m from the bridge is another bridge. Cross back onto the S bank of the river.

10 Follow the path along the S bank, climbing above the water as it becomes a comparatively substantial track, curving round to the R. (800m from the last bridge)

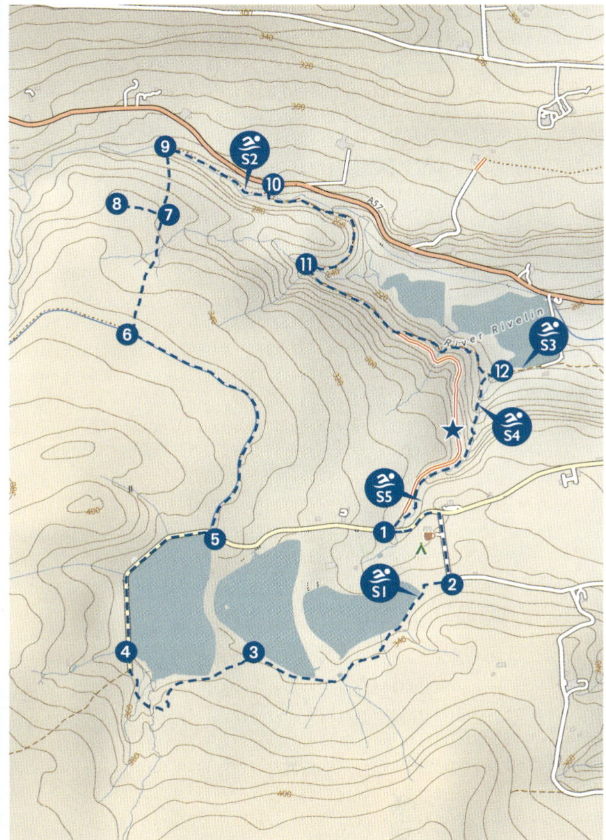

11 Continue on the wide gravel track, keeping L and ignoring any R forks or options until you arrive at a signpost on the R to Wyming Brook Nature Reserve. (1.1km) At 50m past the bottom of Wyming Brook is an access point to Rivelin Reservoir, where an unobserved swim can be enjoyed **S3**.

12 Turn R to begin climbing steeply up wooden steps into the woods alongside Wyming Brook. Follow the braided paths all the way back up the valley, with the water predominantly to your L but on the R towards the top. There is lots of water potential in small plunge pools and waterfalls **S4**, and shallow paddling in dammed-pools **S5** just before you arrive back at the car park. (1km with 85m of height gain)

BAMFORD EDGE
& STEPPING STONES

Tolkienesque ancient woodland, one of England's steepest roads, incredible reservoir views from Bamford Edge and Victorian stepping stones combine to make an excellent outing.

England's textile mills, once the workshop of the world, were the original Northern Powerhouse. They're fundamental to the history, culture and landscape of Northern England. Bamford has an interesting history. It was included in the Domesday Book and remained a small agricultural village until the water-powered corn mill burned down in the late 18th century. After it was rebuilt, it was sold and converted into a cotton-spinning mill. The village was further developed with the building of the three reservoirs' dams and workings upstream: Ladybower, Derwent and Howden. Up to 2,000 workers lived locally, largely in tin-roofed sheds, with many of the inhabitants of the villages of Ashopton and Derwent, which were inundated as the reservoirs were filled, rehoused in Yorkshire Bridge and Bamford. Lots of the families still live locally. The mill is now a very attractive residential building with enviable views across a beautiful weir.

As well as having a rich industrial heritage, Bamford lies on the train line between Sheffield and Manchester; is close to the A57 (Snake Pass), one of the few road routes between the two major cities; and has a great geographical location among the peaks and eastern edges of the Peak District. It's a gem of a village.

The walk begins and finishes at Bamford Recreation Ground, where there is a small car park. If an event is on and parking is limited, it is possible to park at a large pay & display car park at Yorkshire Bridge, or even at the Angler's Rest in the village, but the walk flows better from the Rec. Leave the car park and head back towards the main road, crossing the Derwent and turning left into and through a small ramshackle junk yard. Follow the main road a short distance to a public footpath which accesses a quiet residential

quarter of the village south of the Mill. If you need an early dip in the river, you can get in the water at the mill **S1**, but we recommend saving it for the return leg. Cross the road in the middle of the village **2** and head up Bamford Clough. Be warned, this is not a walk for the unfit! The clough, which was mysteriously resurfaced in 2021, is possibly the steepest road in the Peak District. Unsuitable for motor vehicles, it has been the site of running and cycling challenges over the years. It packs a punch, climbing 140m over just 600m, an average gradient of nearly 25%! On the plus side there are two welcome benches part way up on which to rest and admire the views while you get your breath back, and it's an excellent way of gaining height quickly.

When you arrive at the road at the top of the clough, cross the stile on the other side and bear right on the public footpath. The moors below Bamford have been the subject of access issues for some time and any restrictions are currently relatively relaxed, but a recent fire in the hot, dry summer of 2020 devastated the area, putting access at risk. Please stick to the main path, which winds up through an abandoned but attractive gritstone quarry **3** before bearing left to join Bamford Edge. Instagram has turned the Edge into something of a phenomenon. Crowds of people flock up the steep hillside for 'that photo' of them perched atop an overhanging promontory of rock with Ladybower Reservoir and Yorkshire Bridge perfectly framed in the background and Win Hill across the other side of the valley. Rock climbing is very popular on the Edge, especially on an evening when sunsets can be spectacular over the water.

Having soaked up the views, it's time to descend back to the valley bottom, which is done via one of the most memorable paths in this book **4**. Initially, we descend steeply through bracken and bilberries before entering what is best described as a Tolkie-

nesque wood, where every surface is adorned with thick moss, and every trunk and branch is twisted and gnarled like witches' hands. Tumbling stone walls and narrow defiles mean that this spot is prettier, if less dramatic, than the Insta hot spot above. Being less visited, it is consequently much more peaceful. Rest a while in the wood; people pay good money for such 'forest bathing'.

Once out of the wood, cross the road below, adjacent to the dam wall which you then walk across **5**. At the far end of the dam look in awe at the plug hole overflow, which, if flowing, is a thing of terrifying beauty. Turn left to drop down to the River Derwent. Locals hold a theory that the reason the Derwent is so cold is that the water has spent days, possibly weeks or even longer, lying still at the bottom of Ladybower Reservoir before issuing forth from the dam far colder than that on the sun-warmed surface. At this point in its course, just metres from the dam, some hardy swimmers clearly climb the wall to swim in an attractive series of small waterfalls and pools, but access is not officially allowed. Instead, climb back up to the disused railway line, now a popular walking and cycling route up the valley **6**, to return to Bamford and its mill. The section of river above the mill has a series of delightful picnic spots, some with rope swings **S2**, but be warned that the water is frigid! Swimming can also be enjoyed at the mill itself, either before crossing the arrangement of bridges and stepping stones in another series of falls and pools or, once crossed, in the shallow calm of the weir **S1**.

Before leaving the village, it would be remiss not to call at the Angler's Rest, a community success story. The building was on the verge of being bought by developers to be turned into more housing before the village joined forces to buy it, now running it as a very successful and characterful village pub, café and community space.

1 Park in the small car park next to the park and recreation ground. If it is busy see the alternative parking described in the 'Variants'. Leave the car park and turn R over the bridge over the River Derwent. Turn immediately L once you have crossed the river, into a small scrapyard. Walk through the scrapyard to exit onto the pavement alongside the main road into Bamford village for 100m before taking the footpath on your L into the quiet residential edge of the village. After 200m it is possible to turn L past Bamford Mill to access the main swimming area of the walk **S1**, but unless you are desperate to get into the water, bear R for a further 200m to arrive at the main road in the centre of the village, across from an attractive arrangement of picnic benches under the shade of big leafy trees.

2 Cross the busy road and keep the benches and trees to your L to head up Bamford Clough. Climb STEEPLY up a tarmac track for 600m, ascending 140m in the process! Rest along the way, making the most of the two benches. Keep going all the way to the road. Cross the road and a wooden stile, making sure to bear R on the public footpath. The path bends around to the L via a disused quarry.

3 Head W from the edge of the quarry along a well-used path. Follow this for 500m before trending L to descend and then traverse 150m to Bamford Edge, with outstanding views over Yorkshire Bridge and Ladybower Reservoir. Follow the main path for 1.4km to the T-junction. Turn L to head steeply downhill towards Bamford village.

4 Descend through ancient woods, past stone walls, and back underneath the Edge. The path bends R after 700m before crossing under power lines and forking L into a beech wood. Descend through the wood to reach the busy main road.

5 Cross the road and then follow the path across the top of the dam wall. At the end turn L on the tarmac track, forking L after 200m to descend to the River Derwent. Once you join the road, take the footpath on the R immediately after the sharp bend (in the road) to climb a short way back up to the disused railway track.

6 This track runs straight and level. Follow it for 1.3km, crossing the road at one point to a distinct set of steps dropping off to the L into a field. Descend to the field to then follow the farm track, through a couple of gates, to an open meadow which borders the river. Picnic and swim spots adorn this bank **S2**. At the end of the field is Bamford Mill, weir and stepping stones **S1**.

7 From the Mill head uphill for a few metres before turning R to rejoin the route you started on to return to the car 500m away.

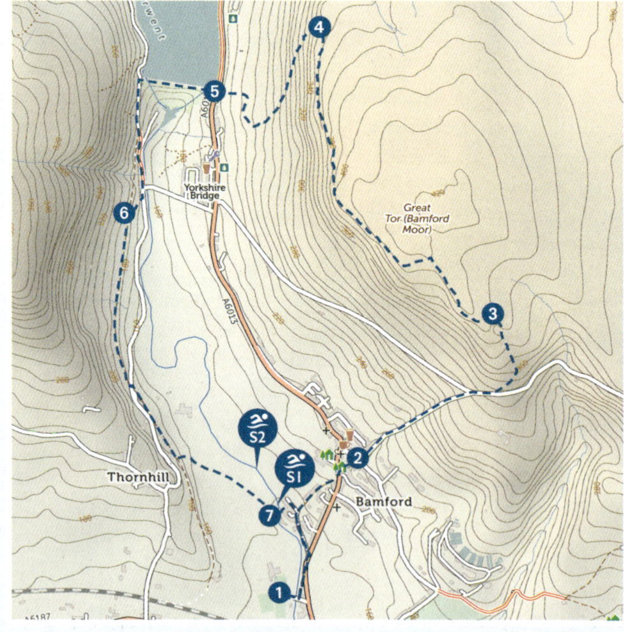

HOPE VALLEY

A short, flat walk from Castleton to Hope and back with lazy swims in the little-frequented Peakshole Water.

The Hope Valley is a lovely part of the world. Just a short hop from Sheffield and Manchester, it is a wide glaciated valley hemmed by steep-sided escarpments. With road access at both ends, it hosts the villages of Edale, Castleton, Hope, Bradwell, Bamford and Hathersage before it bends to the south through Grindleford, Calver, Froggatt, Curbar and Baslow. Throw in the unsightly cement works, built in 1929, before the Peak District was awarded its national park status, and you have a rather confused combination of natural beauty, farming, tourism and industry. Nevertheless, it is comparatively easy to escape and find peace and tranquillity.

Castleton is the honey pot of the Peak District's tourist spots so allow a little extra time to get there and park up in the large pay & display car park **1**. As you walk back through the village, the road twists and turns, as if designed to repel attack, past a melange of gift shops, tearooms and pubs vying for attention. Keep to the main road until almost at the end of the village, where a signed footpath on the right leads into open fields and Peakshole Water. Really just a small stream at this stage, the Peakshole is often mistaken for the upper reaches of the Derwent, which features heavily in this guide. Less than a kilometre from the car park, the Peakshole offers up a gem of a swimming spot: a languid waist-deep pool in a sharp S-bend **S1**. Bounded by sheep-munched grass, it is a quintessential picnic spot. The pool has a shallow beach entry point at the upstream end and is big enough for a decent swim given the stature of the river. Despite its proximity to the village, the road and the cement works, it is a peaceful spot. If you close your eyes and listen, you will hear the murmur of the water as it trickles into and out of the pool, as well as birdsong – but very little

else. It is surprising that such a spot exists so close to the centre of Castleton.

The walk now diverges from the water **2**, through fields via gates and stiles for 500m, crossing a service railway line for the cement works **3** before entering trees as it rejoins the Peakshole at another large S-bend. In fact, there are a series of S-bends, each providing more opportunities, where there are gaps in the fence, to get into the water **S2** + **S3**. The Peakshole now flows along the edge of Hope village; the grounds and buildings of Hope Valley College secondary school are visible through gaps in the foliage. When you reach Pindale Road, turn left to head into the middle of Hope, a quieter and more down-to-earth village with a choice of places to eat and drink, plus public loos.

The return route from Hope to Castleton is convoluted; walls, fences, numerous gates and stiles make it impractical to record turn-by-turn instructions, but if you ensure you don't bear too far to the right, you will keep away from the heights of Lose Hill and you won't go wrong. But if you have the energy and fancy a 360-degree view of the Peak District, the summit of Lose Hill is a fine vantage point and easy enough to climb, with multiple choice routes back down into Castleton and to the car park.

THE ELEPHANT IN THE PARK

Hope Valley Cement Works is a cement plant located between the villages of Hope, Castleton and Bradwell. Visitors to the area are often surprised by the presence of such a factory in the heart of one of the oldest national parks in the world. It started its first full year of production in 1929, well before the national park was created in 1951. Since 1951 most of the outbound traffic from the plant has been exported by rail. The plant is mostly self-contained, with its own shale and limestone quarries adjacent. As it lies inside the Peak District National Park, it is subject to tighter planning restrictions than other cement plants in the UK. It is now the largest cement plant in the UK (in terms of tonnage of cement), and it is also one of the largest emitters of CO_2 within the national park. A study in 2020 determined that the plant supported a total of 270 jobs and brought in over £60 million to the local economy, roughly one tenth of the economic impact of tourism to the park. Permission to continue operation will expire in 2042, when operations are expected to cease.

1 Park in the large pay & display car park at the northern edge of Castleton. Exit and turn L by the mini roundabout. Walk through the village on the main A6187 (Castleton Road) for 600m to a green signpost on the R: 'Public Footpath To Hope, altitude 592 feet', before the road bends sharply to the L. Turn R to follow a well-graded gravel track past a farm on your R to join the Peakshole Water after 200m, as the track becomes a path. Go through a gate to follow the path towards the cement works chimney. Inaccessible at first, the stream opens up, with a fine swimming spot on an exaggerated S-bend after 500m **S1**.

2 Now the footpath diverges from the water to continue almost due E for about 500m, through fields, gates and stiles, crossing the active service railway for the local cement works before rejoining the stream.

3 From the railway crossing, the path follows the water more closely again, with numerous shady and quiet swim spots on its bends **S2** + **S3**. Continue to Pindale Road. (500m total)

4 Turn L on Pindale Road to descend into Hope village. After 300m cross the A6187 in the middle of the village. Turn L to walk past the Curry Cabin, turning R immediately after it (public footpath sign on the R). Follow the narrow footway up steps and through a gate into a housing

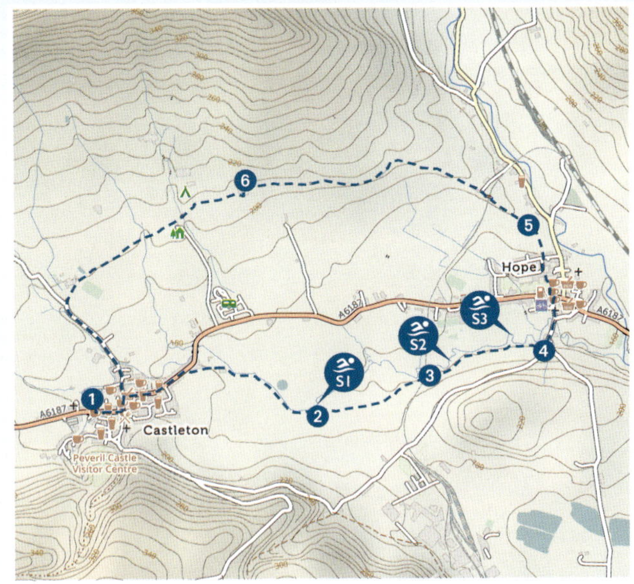

estate, then past Hope Clinic to a field, at the far end of which is a small wooden gate on the edge of the village, signposted 'Lose Hill'.

5 The path now heads NW towards Lose Hill and then W towards Castleton village. Once over the bouncy footbridge over the railway line, the path becomes very narrow, with barely enough space for people to pass each other. There are several gates, but the terrain is relatively flat and easy going. Follow signs to 'Castleton Village' and 'Walks Around Castleton (Walk 2)' arrows. If in doubt, keep L as going R will likely lead you to one of the paths up Lose Hill. About 1.5km after leaving Hope, you will arrive at Spring House Farm Cottages.

6 Turn L and then immediately R (wooden signpost to 'Castleton Village'). Follow a gravel road for 500m, passing the rear of Castleton YHA to reach a metal gate (signposted 'No Footpath'). Go through the stone pinch to its L and follow the gravel path through a field with fine views of Mam Tor and The Great Ridge. Continue along Robinlands Lane (gravel), past the Hollowford Centre, to Hollowford (aka Millbridge) Road (tarmac), which leads back into the centre of Castleton. When you reach the main road in the centre of the village, turn R, retracing your steps from the start of the walk.

Walk 14

HATHERSAGE STEPPING STONES

As well as playing host to one of the country's finest open-air lidos, Hathersage lies on the River Derwent, crossed on our walk on wonky, but not wobbly, stepping stones.

Stepping stones are an ageless and elegant solution to river crossing, requiring no engineering and using materials from the riverbed. They exist in many spots in the Peak District, often having been modernised to make them safer. The stones crossing the Derwent up-river of Hathersage feel like they have been there for millennia; they are wonky, worn and not that easy to cross. And we love them for just that reason. Do bear in mind that if the water level is high, the stones may be impassable, and the described swim spots will probably be too fast flowing to enter safely. If you decide against crossing the stones but want to persevere with the walk, the alternative crossing is described under 'Variants'.

We start the walk from the large pay & display car park in the middle of Hathersage, next to the open-air lido. If you can time your visit with public opening hours, then a visit to the lido would be a fine complementary activity for the other half of your day. With views of Stanage Edge, it's hard to imagine an open-air heated pool with a better backdrop. Follow the directions through the village (**1** – **3** and **S1**), picking up provisions from Harrington Butchers, who make the best pies in the valley, if you need sustenance along the way. Once out of Hathersage, the walk follows the River Derwent first up-river **4** + **S2**, and then once across the stones **S3** back down **5** as far as the B6001 between Hathersage and Grindleford **6**. The river has a decent flow at most of the spots where you can access it, so make sure you know where to get out before you get in, and wear something on your feet as it is impossible to see the riverbed through the dark water. Swim spots abound, mainly on the return leg, back downriver. It

is rarely deep, but explore and you will find plenty of potential for a good swim against the current. Sitting a while by the Stepping Stones can be entertaining viewing, as walkers sometimes work in teams to help each other across the unfamiliar terrain; none of the gaps between stones are bigger than a large stride, but the rushing water beneath your legs can be somewhat disorientating.

Where the walk reaches the road between Hathersage and Grindleford there is one final swim spot **S4** immediately up-river (with potential also immediately downriver if you walk under the arches of the bridge). Entry is next to the stone embankment, where the water quickly deepens to about 2m, deep enough for you to jump carefully from the stone embankment (check the depth first). If you need a drink and a rest from walking before returning to your vehicle, The Plough Inn, just a couple of hundred metres down the road towards Grindleford, has a delightful beer garden, often with live music, which catches the late evening sun. As you return into Hathersage, David Mellor's cutlery shop, workshop and café are also well worth a visit as you pass by.

1 Park in the large pay & display car park in the centre of Hathersage, next to the lido. If parking in Hathersage is difficult, there is a large lay-by 200m from the crossing point on the A6187 towards Hope, which is convenient for this walk (start following directions from the road crossing in point 4 below). Turn R out of the car park to walk S down Oddfellows Road to the main road (B6001/Station Road). Turn R. After 150m turn L at a small green public footpath sign next to the bus stop before the Little John Hotel. Follow the footpath for 40m to Mill Lane. Turn L and follow Mill Lane for 250m, underneath the high stone arches of the railway line, to another green public footpath sign on the R by the green doors of The Music Mill.

2 Turn R at The Music Mill, immediately crossing a bridge over a stream. There is a potential swim/dipping spot on your R underneath the railway arches **S1**. Follow the footpath through the field to the far corner and pass through a gate to meet the main A6187 (Castleton Road). Turn R to walk briefly back towards Hathersage, underneath the bridge, before crossing the road to take the R fork by the Sladen Lodge signpost. Follow the narrow path, between metal fences and stone walls, steeply uphill for 100m to join Jagger's Lane. Turn L and walk along Jagger's Lane for 250m to a metal gate, stone pinch and wooden public footpath sign on the L.

3 Go through the pinch between the stones and descend diagonally through the field to the railway crossing. Cross with caution before continuing in the same direction on the other side to meet and cross the busy A6187. Go through the gap in the hedge on the far side of the road by the wooden public footpath sign and walk diagonally through the field towards the River Derwent (200m from the road). Follow the footpath up-river, keeping close to the bank. The first good swim spot is on the L around 160m after joining the river, marked by a dilapidated wooden bench **S2**. The water is waist deep and quite fast flowing. Continue through a gate for a further 200m up-river to the Stepping Stones, marked by a curious wooden structure seemingly randomly located in the middle of the field!

4 Cross the Stepping Stones (see alternative route notes under 'Variants' if crossing them is impractical). There is another good swim spot up-river of the stones **S3**. On the far bank climb the steps and turn L. The path now follows the river closely all the way back to the B6001 (Hathersage to Grindleford road). This section is 2.2km long, with many gates and several small, narrow bridges to navigate, passing through Goose Nest Wood towards the end and numerous picnic spots by the river.

5 There is a good swim spot immediately where the B6001 crosses the Derwent **S4**, with jumping possible from the stone wall 25m up-river from the bridge. (Check the depth first!) Turn L on the B6001 and follow the pavement for 800m, past David Mellor's cutlery shop, into Hathersage. Turn R on Oddfellows Lane to return to your vehicle.

WATERFALL SWALLET & BRETTON CLOUGH

Waterfall Swallett is unique in these parts: a hole in the ground into which a waterfall flows, just a short hop from the infamous 'Plague Village' of Eyam.

Much has been written about Eyam. Few people venture far out of the village to the adjacent, alien landscape of Bretton Clough; still fewer have delved into the otherworldly Waterfall Swallet. This walk takes in all three, linking them in a challenging 12.5km loop starting and ending in Eyam, giving plenty of opportunity after the walk to explore Riley's Graves, the Vinegar Stones and, if time allows, the museum, should your curiosity get the better of you.

Parking in Eyam ❶ is free and spacious. Do please consider visiting one of the tearooms, cafés or pubs to support the community. Be aware that for the middle section of the walk you will be out of mobile reception. Navigating from a paper map is tricky due to the undulating nature of the terrain; you may want to have some offline maps downloaded onto a digital device.

From the car park head into the village past the well-kept church. Leave the churchyard and walk along the main street. You will see a curious contraption on your right; it's a sheep-roasting device! The most popular time of the year to visit Eyam is the last week of August, during Carnival Week: the streets are garlanded with colourful bunting as the Annual Sheep Roast takes place, and the village is thronged with thousands of visitors. If you are here during that time (assuming you have found somewhere to park), rest assured that the footpaths you will be treading will be largely empty.

Continue past Eyam Hall, a 17th-century family manor house with a walled garden, before leaving the main street ❷ to pass through a less visited part of the village to access

INFORMATION

DISTANCE: 12.5km
TIME: 5–6 hours
MAP: OS Explorer OL24 The Peak District – White Peak Area
PARKING: Free public car park in Eyam (SK 216 767; 53.2869, -1.6764)
PUBLIC TRANSPORT: 257 bus between Sheffield and Bakewell
SWIMMING: Waterfall Swallet **S1**, Stoke Ford **S2**
PLACES OF INTEREST: Eyam – historic plague village with museums, tearooms and pubs; Waterfall Swallet; The Barrel Inn; Bretton Clough; Sir William Hill
REFRESHMENTS: Tearooms, pubs and shop in Eyam; The Barrel Inn halfway around
VARIANTS: If you have time after the walk, pay a visit to the museum in Eyam and explore the historic 'Plague Village'.

rolling green fields studded with majestic, lone sycamore trees. The farmland is typical of this area, subdivided into a hodgepodge of randomly shaped fields bounded by limestone walls. The footpath traces a fairly plumb line through these fields to arrive at the quiet B road between the villages of Eyam and Foolow.

A short way down the road towards Foolow is our first swim spot **SI** – Waterfall Swallet **4**. The swallet is a tree-lined sinkhole, where water flowing across impermeable shale falls from the disused Bretton tin mines as a spectacular waterfall. The water disappears into fissures in the limestone at the bottom of the depression. During times of flood, this area fills with water and overflows into the nearby Waterfall Hole Cave. Conversely, during times of drought, the waterfall can be just a damp cliff. While there is no plunge

pool at its base, the cascade provides a great cold shower on a hot day. In fact, it's one of the Peak District's finest waterfalls when flowing well.

Once you've showered, climb carefully back out of the hole the way you came in, and retrace the route back up the road towards Eyam. Although it's a quiet road, it's narrow and the pavement is narrower still so take care. A left turn off the road leads to a rather incongruous stone-processing factory. Ignore the footpath signs directing you through the yard, as these would take you back to Eyam. An alternative path skirts around the left-hand side. If you are there during working hours, a friendly chap in a high-vis jacket may well help you politely on your way.

The path from the top left-hand corner of the factory is delightful. During spring the yellow gorse bushes and swathes of bluebells are a riot of fragrant, rural colour. The climb passes quickly enough in these surroundings, to bring you to Sir William Hill Road **5**, just uphill from The Barrel Inn, Derbyshire's highest pub (365m). If there is a pub in the Peak District with a finer outlook, we've yet to find it. The traditional Derbyshire country inn dates back to 1597 and stands at the head of Bretton Clough. You will definitely feel like you've earned a drink stop here, so rest a while and take in the views to the south. Things are about to change dramatically.

Beyond The Barrel a private track takes you north with views of the earlier part of the walk, out over the eastern gritstone edges of Higger Tor, Millstone, Stanage, Bamford and Derwent, and further still to Bleaklow and Kinder. If you are here during the late summer and start early, you could be treated to a spectacular cloud inversion, common at that time of year. Leaving the track, we pass through a small farmstead and into a large field. Head down through the field before dropping steeply down a gully and some steep steps into the clough itself **6**. Bretton Clough is a remarkable Peak District valley; a glance at a map shows a most unusual confusion of contour lines. Landslips have caused a series of curious landscape features, which you would be forgiven for mistaking for glacial drumlins! While the landslips of Alport Castles and Mam Tor are nationally famous, Bretton Clough is barely known and yet provides some outstanding scenery. A trip down here in the snow offers some extreme sledging challenges!

The brook itself is out of bounds, hidden below a fence and largely out of sight. Choose any of the myriad paths down the clough, keeping close to the fence on your left, and you will end up at Stoke Ford **7**, where the Bretton Brook meets Highlow Brook. Here is our second cooling-off spot **S2**. Sadly, there is not enough water for a proper swim, but some visitors have built dams at the confluence, forming pools which are sometimes deep enough to immerse oneself. Deer and pheasant frequent the clough, so keep an eye on your dog if you have one.

After cooling off and picnicking, retrace the route for a short way before breaking off to the left for a long but steady and beautiful climb back up **8**, to the summit of Sir William Hill (429m). Writing in 1881, Edward Bradbury called Sir William 'one of the most stately and personal hills in the Peak'. With its radio mast on the summit, it is one of the most prominent landmarks in the area yet sees but a fraction of the traffic of neighbouring summits. No bad thing if you've got this far. Summertime sees the ground covered in the regal vivid purple of the

heather, with juicy bilberries ripe for the picking.

From the summit **9** we follow the Roman Road, a broken track still braved by the occasional adventurous motorist, which crests the summit of the hill before crossing it to descend ever more steeply back into Eyam **10** and the bustle of this historic village. If you have time, a trip to the museum is highly recommended, where you can pick up a map of the village and visit the likes of 'Riley Graves', six gravestones and a tomb, enclosed by a stone wall, where the entire Hancock family were buried in 1666 having succumbed to the plague; and the 'Vinegar Stones', where locals would leave provisions for the quarantined and starving villagers, who would in turn leave coins as payment in depressions filled with vinegar to disinfect the money and prevent the disease spreading.

1 From the public car park in Eyam, head for the SE corner and follow a gravel footpath into the village, past a playground on your L and then a football pitch on your R. Just after the football pitch turn sharp R by a black litter bin. Follow this path into the churchyard to continue in front of the church onto the main street through the village. Turn R. Continue along the main street for 200m to turn L onto New Close. (600m total)

2 Follow New Close, going straight on whenever there is a choice, for 600m before you enter open fields just after Windmill Lane and then Tideswell Lane. Continue across fields for 1km to a gate in a wall next to a 7ft-high wooden signpost.

3 Turn R at the signpost to follow a farm track, through a metal 7-bar gate (make sure you shut it properly), between two walls to the road between Eyam and Foolow. (200m) Turn L and follow the narrow pavement on the L side of the road for nearly 200m, past a house on your R. Opposite the farm on your L there is a track by a round mirror. Follow this track for just a few metres to a small wooden gate on your L. Go through the gate and descend steep, rocky steps into a large hollow. At the bottom, on the far side, is Waterfall Swallet **S1**.

4 Ascend the way you came, back through the gate and onto the road, and back to where you

joined the road. Continue past the junction for another 300m to turn L towards a large working mineral-refining plant. Ignore the footpath signs through the works (these would take you back to Eyam); instead, keep L to skirt around the L-hand side, past a fenced-off pond. From the top L-hand corner of the works, trend diagonally NW through fields and gorse bushes, past white fingerposts, to eventually arrive, after a fairly steep climb, at a tarmac road just uphill from The Barrel Inn. (1.9km total)

5 Turn L, uphill, along Sir William Hill Road. Immediately past the pub, turn R. After 400m down this lane take the footpath through the grounds of a house and farm to emerge onto open fields. Head for the bottom L corner of the field, then into a narrow gully before climbing briefly and steeply back up and R to a stile. From here follow steep earth-and-wood steps down into Bretton Clough.

6 The brook in the bottom of the clough is fenced off, and there is a maze of paths to choose from. Don't worry too much about the one you take but keep as close to the fence above the brook as you can, moving in a NE direction. After 1.5km of undulating and tricky terrain you will arrive at Stoke Ford, marked by a large green footpath sign (No 99) **S2**.

7 After cooling off in the ford, briefly retrace your steps for around 100m before taking the L

fork in the path. After a further 50m or so the path bends sharply L before bending back R to continue in a SW direction, almost parallel to the route down to the ford. At 800m from the ford the path again turns 90 degrees L, following a high stone wall on the L, past a striking outcrop of gritstone on the R, to an unusually shaped metal gate and a high stone wall and stile after 300m.

8 On the other side of the wall is another distinctive green footpath sign (No 457). Take the middle option signposted 'Eyam'. Follow the single track through the heather and bilberry scrub, uphill all the way, to the summit of Sir William Hill and trig point. (1.2km)

9 From the summit head due E, downhill alongside the wall, for 300m to a stile in the wall. Cross this onto the broken road. Cross the road to another stile, then cross this into open fields. Follow the footpath through the fields for 600m to a tarmac road. Dogleg L to cross the road. Follow the footpath above a beech wood (on your R) SE for 400m to Edge Road above Eyam.

10 Follow the footpath SW, down towards Eyam, for 500m until you reach the track by which you originally left the car park at the start of the walk. Turn R to go around the football field and back to the car park.

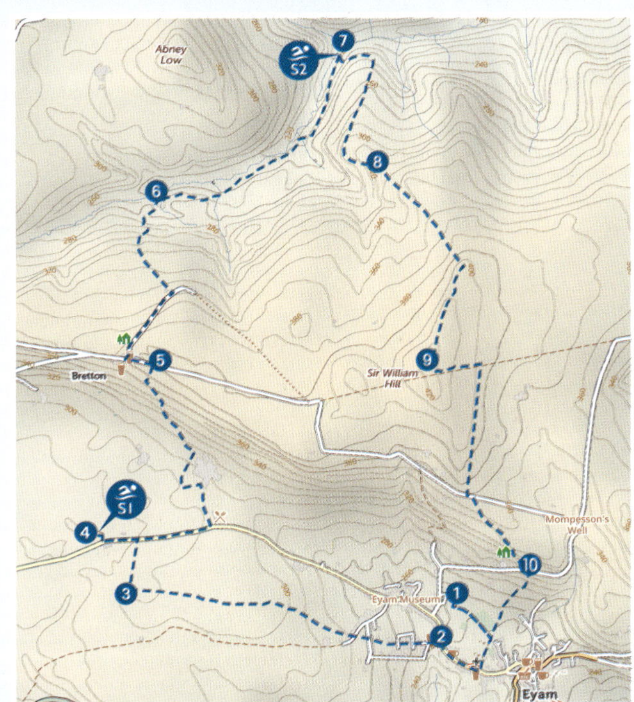

Abney
Low
Bretton
Sir William
Hill
Mompesson's
Well
Eyam Museum
Eyam

GRINDLEFORD DERWENT & PADLEY GORGE

One of the finest swim-walks in the Peak District, this route takes in the tangled beauty of Padley Gorge, with delightful picnic and swim spots along the River Derwent.

The walk begins at St Helen's Church in the village of Grindleford. Just 20 minutes from Sheffield by bus, train or car, it's a popular village but without the outdoor shops and cafés, so remains relatively sleepy. The church houses an impressive, volunteer-run community shop tucked away in the side chapel, which serves hot drinks and freshly baked cakes at very sensible prices. It is, incidentally, surprisingly well stocked with a wide range of worthwhile products, an excellent enterprise run by the villagers. It's a great place to meet friends, begin your walk and treat yourselves to an ice cream at the finish or the start – or even both!

Begin by following a small access lane to the right side of the church to the lower edge of Hay Wood ❷. A calm atmosphere pervades these woods. Just a hundred metres or so after you have entered the shade of the trees, a faint path leads off to the right to an open area beneath some towering beech trees. This is known as 'The Cathedral', and locals have put up a mighty rope swing. There's also a very small pool here, which youngsters may want to play in **S1**. Deer from the nearby Chatsworth Estate regularly frequent the wood and have created an intricate and extensive network of pathways and trods. Go quietly and there's a very good chance you will spot some.

At the top of the wood ❸, where the ground levels out, the heavier canopy thins to birch, with an underlayer of verdant bracken. During the summer months this area is not a place to linger as the ground literally teams with large wood ants. Emerging from the birch onto open land, you're treated to a fine 360-degree view over Grindleford, the Hope Valley, Sir William Hill, Abney

INFORMATION

DISTANCE: 8.3km
TIME: 2–3 hours
MAP: OS Explorer OL24 The Peak District – White Peak Area
PARKING: St Helen's Church, Grindleford; roadside parking; alternatively, park in the pay & display bays by Grindleford station and begin the walk from direction point 11 (SK 245 778; 53.2974, -1.6331)
PUBLIC TRANSPORT: Trains from Manchester and Sheffield; 65 and 257 buses from Sheffield
SWIMMING: Hay Wood shallow kids dip **S1**, Padley Gorge pools **S2** + **S3** and numerous spots on the River Derwent **S4** + **S5**
PLACES OF INTEREST: Grindleford Community Shop, ice cream vans at Padley Gorge, Grindleford Station Café, Millwheel picnic spot
REFRESHMENTS: Grindleford Community Shop, Sir William Hotel, The Grouse Inn, Padley Gorge ice cream vans, Grindleford Station Café (cash only)
VARIANTS: Extend the walk up to Longshaw Estate (National Trust), with further hidden pools in the Burbage Valley beyond. For a shorter walk, arrange a drop-off or start at the ice cream vans at Padley Gorge (direction point 8) and simply do the second half (ice cream vans to St Helen's Church is approx 3km)

Can be combined with Walk 17 – Froggatt Edge & Bridges

Moor, Hathersage, Stanage Edge, Millstone Edge and White Edge **4**.

The walk now strikes northward, through an expansive open meadow, another favourite haunt of the deer, before hugging the edge of the woods. Just before reaching Yarncliffe Quarry **8** (Note that legend has it that if you utter the word 'Yarncliffe' aloud it will rain later that day...), on the left-hand side, you will spot ancient stone steps descending steeply towards a cliff edge. Follow these down, nip between a boulder and the edge and you will find the Quarryman's Kitchen, an overhang set into the cliff, with a stone seat and table hewn from the rock. The view over the woods is sublime, and it's not difficult to imagine quarrymen of old enjoying a few minutes of peace over their lunch.

Now to Padley Gorge. There are two different ways to tackle it; both are rocky and can be muddy. Follow the steps in the route description to enjoy the traditional experience, at the cost of the crowds by the ice cream vans **9**. Alternatively, if you prefer comparative peacefulness, descend to the riverbed itself. If you are sufficiently sure-footed and adventurous, a delightful hour can be spent boulder hopping, balancing along fallen tree trunks and plunging into river pools **S2** + **S1**. As you adventure your way to the bottom, you are unlikely to meet anyone else. You will be entranced to discover how magical this area is considering its proximity to busy, bustling Sheffield. Towards the bottom of the gorge is a river bridge and tunnel, a fun place to slide and play. Occasionally, small creatures become trapped in the confines. A grateful toad and slow-worm were lifted to freedom on one occasion.

If you need a loo or seek refreshments, Grindleford Station Café **11** is infamous for its grumpy staff and inflexible menu, but it does make very good eggs and chips. Take note that payment is cash only. Leaving the station, the route passes through Nether Padley, home to a community of artists, authors and poets. Fresh greenhouse and garden produce is often laid out on garden walls on a select-and-trust-pay system. Padley Chapel is worth a minor detour to read about a grisly local murder.

Departing from the village, you will see several gritstone mill wheels hewn from Bole Hill Quarry. The sharp-eyed may spot an unnatural terrain anomaly on the left. Earth removed when the four-mile-long Totley railway towards Sheffield was excavated was dumped here way back in 1893. Bole Hill Quarry also provided much of the stone used to build the dams at Ladybower, Howden and Derwent reservoirs.

The walk is now in its final stage, returning along the bank of the River Derwent. The source of the Derwent is a mere 16–24 kilometres away, but it is already a mature river, wide, deep in places and slow-moving, its placid flow interrupted by a series of small, broken weirs which provide excellent swimming spots (**S4** + **S5**, ignore the fishing signs, but be sensitive and friendly if you do encounter anglers). The flanking woods and banks are habitat for a pleasantly wide variety of bird life. It is not uncommon to see the electric blue flash of a resident kingfisher. Anglers and bathers frequent this section between the villages of Hathersage and Grindleford. The grassy banks provide numerous classic picnic spots to sit, relax, maybe even sunbathe, and then swim in peaceful deep pools.

Do try to factor in a final visit to the Grindleford Community Shop in the village church for some homemade produce, excellent coffee, ice cream or garden-fresh fruit and vegetables. I'm allowed to sing its praises – I live in Grindleford! And it genuinely is a lovely area.

1 Leave the car parked on the roadside near St Helen's Church and walk up the unpaved track to the E/R of the church. After 200m the track bends R into the grounds of a private residence. Go through the adjoining gateway on the L and enter Hay Wood.

2 Continue straight up, and 100m after a gate on the R, tucked away 50m from the path, there is a mighty rope swing and a very small pool **S1**. Continue for a further 700m on a rough, often steep footpath. Whenever you are faced with an option, always choose the steepest one. Eventually, bear R to enter a steep gully, ducking under two tree branches. At the top of the gully ascent, turn back sharply L onto a minor path.

3 Follow this for 200m, through birch trees then bracken, skirting past a quarried pinnacle, which is hidden on the L, and a large gritstone cairn. This, the highest point of the walk, provides a superb view over Grindleford village and the Hope Valley.

4 Continue in the same direction, bearing R as you descend to the walled corner of a field with a wooden kissing gate. (100m) There is a black plastic pipe protecting a cable by the gate.

5 Walk through the field, heading due N, for 300m. Go through a second gate in the stone wall and turn R to walk, at first, between two walls, then very steeply downward to a small stream. Cross this and bear R (NE). When you come to a crossroads, take the middle option and ignore the other two paths which follow another stream.

6 Follow the footpath into the woods, keeping fields close by on your R-hand side, for 600m to a fork as you approach the end of the fields.

7 Take the L fork, descending 400m towards the main road. Cross this at a gated entrance into Yarncliffe Quarry. Across the road are stone steps set into the wall. Climb over these and enter into the woods of Padley Gorge.

8 Turn R, climbing through the woods, and follow any one of the braided paths between the road and the river for 600m. Here, at the edge of the woods, is a popular picnic spot, with close-by roadside parking and ice cream vans. There are two wooden bridges over the river.

9 Cross either of these and follow the river downstream. Ignore the R-hand fork in 700m. After a further 200m take the L-hand fork, which zigzags downhill to another wooden bridge. Several shallow pools and waterfalls here are favourite spots for a splash on a warm day **S2** + **S3**.

⑩ Cross the bridge. The river is now to your R. Descend for 400m, resisting the opportunity to bear L away from the river. A stone wall is reached. Go through the gate in the wall to join a tarmac track/road.

⑪ If you wish to make a detour to the station café, it is 50m away to the L, over the railway bridge; however, the route turns R. Follow the road, which quickly turns into an unpaved track, for 800m, passing private houses, a National Trust barn and the historic Padley Chapel. Just as you exit the woods, a pathway leads away from the track on the L.

⑫ Take this path for 300m, heading downhill and over the railway line. Immediately on the R is another kissing gate. Go through the kissing gate.

⑬ Follow the footpath, which runs parallel with but drops below the railway line, downhill for 300m to arrive at the River Derwent. Turn L along the river and continue for 500m to another gate at the edge of the woods.

⑭ Follow the footpath through fields along the riverbank for 1.5km, crossing a minor concrete bridge a little way from the river. There are lots of swimming opportunities along the river, with the broken weirs usually regarded as the best spots **S4** + **S5**. The footpath leads back to our starting point at St Helen's Church.

FROGGATT EDGE & BRIDGES

This exhilarating outing along Froggatt Edge visits a secret waterfall, followed by a descent to the lazily flowing River Derwent.

Grindleford is the first village on the train line out of Sheffield and is also served by buses from the city, and from Bakewell to the south. It beckons walkers and swimmers looking for access to the River Derwent. You can start the walk from the village, but if you are travelling by car, the best start point is at Hay Wood car park, in a shady wooded area set back from the road. Head south, crossing a small stream **1** before crossing the road and joining the permissive bridleway following the top of Froggatt Edge. This route is usually busy with walkers and families on bikes; it is comparatively flat with grand picnic spots and great expansive views **2**.

Froggatt Edge is one of many local sedimentary gritstone outcrops revealed as softer overlays have been weathered away by the elements. It is conjectured that a single vast river flowing from the north deposited this material as part of a vast alluvial fan. Massive gritstone boulders lie where they have fallen, and silver birch, oak and ash woods have colonised the areas between, the ground beneath carpeted with wild flowers as spring arrives. The higher ground hosts bracken and bilberry, positively glowing golden against the rocky backdrop as summer turns to autumn.

A little way along the path, just before you reach the 'Edge', there is a big wooden gate next to a small stream. Follow the stream **3** downhill for a lovely surprise. Completely hidden from passers-by on the main track is a 3m-high waterfall. It's tricky to get down to, requiring sure-footedness, but once there it's possible to stand right underneath it for a glorious natural shower **S1**. Afterwards, simply retrace your steps up to the track and continue, passing through the gate.

INFORMATION

DISTANCE: 8.4km
TIME: 3–4 hours
MAP: OS Explorer OL24 The Peak District – White Peak Area
PARKING: Hay Wood car park; National Trust pay & display (SK 255 776; 53.2954, -1.6181)
PUBLIC TRANSPORT: Trains from Manchester and Sheffield; 65 and 271 buses from Sheffield to Grindleford
SWIMMING: Waterfall on Froggatt Edge **S1**, lots of swim spots along the River Derwent **S2** + **S3** + **S5** + **S6**, with big jumping potential from the bridge **S4**
REFRESHMENTS: The Grouse Inn, The Chequers Inn, Grindleford Community Shop
VARIANTS: From New Bridge (see direction point **6**) continue along the L bank of the river for 200m to the weir for a lovely picnic spot.

If Froggatt Edge is too busy when you visit, consider walking the close-by alternative, White Edge, which runs parallel with Froggatt but is higher, wilder, rougher and much quieter. Oh, and it offers even better views

Can be combined with Walk 16 – Grindleford Derwent & Padley Gorge

The next section is one of the most scenic. The trees thin out and views open up: White Edge and Big Moor are to the left and Hope Valley is to the right. A healthy herd of wild deer graze on Big Moor and in the woods, so the chances are you will see them. Look out for the stone circle on the left, a little way after the gate; it's set back from the track about 30m. Adders are not uncommon, often seen curled up, basking in the sun. Never aggressive, they will glide away silently as they sense the faint tremor of your approach.

Shortly before leaving the track, you will come across a cluster of large gritstone boulders to the right, just perfect for scrambles and a great picnicking spot. At 200m past these boulders a pathway breaks down to the left to head back up to Froggatt Edge. Walking back along the foot of the cliffs, you will almost certainly see climbers. Now look for a very rocky path that drops down from the edge just before the imposing Valkyrie pinnacle, the impressive rocky prow towering above you **4**.

Froggatt Edge is named because of its proximity to Froggatt village nestling below it. About 200 years ago the Duke of Rutland, the landowner, built 17 cottages for his workers. Some of those cottages still stand, now listed buildings. The more recent, grander buildings were commissioned by wealthy business owners who, understandably, aspired to live in this magnificent rural idyll while still remaining close to the factories entombed in the dark, polluted metropolises of Sheffield and Chesterfield. Walking a little way through the village, you will come across a hole in the wall and an ancient stone stile leading down to the River Derwent **6** + **7**.

The stretch of river below the bridge is a popular swim spot, which has led to some conflict with residents, mostly because of inconsiderate parking. Although it is possible to swim here, we really do ask you to consider moving downriver a little, to one of dozens of great spots immediately by the path **S2** + **S3**, **5**. The entry points lie across the river on the opposite bank **S5** + **S6**; you will return that way shortly. These swim spots are more open to the sun and have handy picnic spots in the fields close by. Please note that there are water voles living along the banks of this section of river, so don't disturb the vegetation and only enter the water at the obvious points. The walk turn-around spot is at New Bridge, a little way up-river from

a prominent weir, where the river widens out to form a pool. The bridge parapet is a particularly popular jumping spot, 5m above the river, and the water is a comforting 3–4m deep directly below the centre of the bridge **S4**. Always check the depth before jumping in case of submerged branches. Be wary of traffic on the bridge as it squeezes past jumpers awaiting their turn. Close to the bridge, on the other bank, is a signposted wildlife reserve, providing sanctuary for the great crested newt, and, as already mentioned, endangered water voles live in the riverbank.

Back in Froggatt village, now on the other bank, cross the graceful stone bridge. Turn left through the village, eventually leaving the tarmac to follow a walled track paved with great gritstone slabs quarried from Stoke Quarry across the river **8**. The path now crosses open fields. If you are passing as dusk approaches, do look out for the barn owl who lives in the barn just before entering Hay Wood. The last dipping spot on the route, known as the 'Gruffalo Pond' **S7**, lies 100m into the woods, but due to its shallow depth, it seems to appeal only to young children and dogs, despite its picture-perfect location **9**.

The path crosses another open field, on the edge of Grindleford village. It is owned by a local tropical butterfly house, who have invested a great deal of effort into several conservation and restoration projects. The local flora and fauna are described on interesting, informative signs, and you will see bird boxes, which attract owls and other species of birdlife. From the end of the field follow the track and then the footpath past St Helen's Church and head up through Hay Wood back to the car park **10**.

Refreshments and loos are all quite close to the route, but none lie directly on it. The Grouse Inn is a short distance from the car park, accessible by a footpath running diagonally across the fields to the northeast. The Chequers Inn is on the main A625, about 50m from where the route crosses on the descent from Froggatt Edge. A hostelry in some form has stood on this site for well over five hundred years! And lastly, located in the side chapel of St Helen's Church, before your return to the car park, is the Grindleford Village Community Shop: a delightful shop and basic café serving hot drinks and home-baked cakes at sensible prices.

THE NATIONAL TRUST
HORSE HAY COPPICE
PLEASE HELP
THE NATIONAL TRUST
TO CARE FOR THIS PROPERTY
BY NOT LEAVING LITTER,
LIGHTING FIRES OR
DAMAGING TREES OR PLANTS
AND KEEPING YOUR DOGS
UNDER CLOSE CONTROL
SEE BYLAWS ON THE BACK OF THIS NOTICE

1 Head S out of the car park. Immediately drop down a steep stone track and cross a stream on stepping stones. Climb steeply up the path and steps to a gate and cross the A625. Bear R and go through a wooden gate. (100m)

2 Follow the 4x4 track uphill at first, passing a large lone boulder on the R, and continue, now along the flat, for 900m to a gate at a crossing of a small stream.

3 Bear away from the track onto the minor pathway to the R, following the stream downhill for 50m to a hidden waterfall. This requires a proper scramble to access. In all but the hottest summers there is enough flow for a worthwhile shower **S1**. Once back on the main track, continue S for 900m along the top of Froggatt Edge, with lovely views down the Hope Valley. About 100m past a collection of large (3–4m tall) boulders on your R, turn sharply R on a rocky track that leads back on itself, under the edge.

4 Follow the end of Froggatt Edge for 150m and perhaps pause for a moment to watch the climbers. A very rocky path drops steeply down to the L just before the prominent Valkyrie Pinnacle.

5 Scramble carefully down the rocky pathway between birch trees, down into the wood below. Cross over a prominent,

wide, flat pathway after 200m, passing through the wooden gate, then cross the A625 after a further 300m (You will see The Chequers Inn 100m up the road to the R.) before descending to the road in Froggatt village after a further 200m. Turn R on the road and walk towards the centre of the village for 100m to a 'hole' and stile in the stone wall on your L, about 50m before the bridge in the centre of the village. (800m in total)

6 Follow the riverside path S for 1.3km, past numerous swimming opportunities in the River Derwent **S2** + **S3**, to arrive at New Bridge, just 100m upstream from Calver Weir. Jumping is possible from the bridge on the up-river side in the middle **S4**. It is popular locally.

7 Cross over the bridge and turn R immediately on the far side and follow the path back up-river (turning R at the fork after 100m), with even more swimming opportunities, accessing the river from the other side. This side is less shady, with picnicking possible in the adjacent fields **S5** + **S6**. (900m)

8 At Froggatt, turn R over the classically graceful bridge and turn L through the village. The road climbs gently uphill. As it bends, bear L onto a walled, cobblestoned lane past the last houses in the village. Go through the field, doglegging R and then L, to enter Hay Wood. (1.1km)

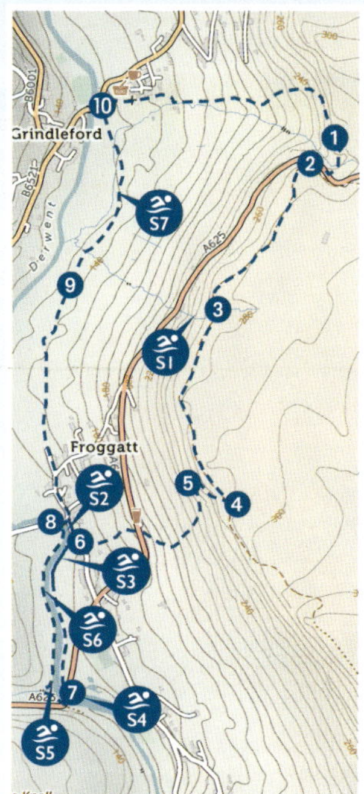

9 Follow the paved path as it winds, climbs and dips through the woods, past an idyllic pool which is, sadly, only deep enough for kids to paddle in **S7**. The path eventually leaves the wood and heads across an open field to join the B6521 in Grindleford. (900m)

10 Turn R up a 4x4 track by St Helen's Church and follow it for 100m until it enters Hay Wood. Follow the footpath all the way up through the wood, always taking the steepest option, to arrive back at the car park after 1.2km.

WHITE EDGE

A wild moorland walk among herds of free-roaming feral deer with a surprising number of swim spots.

Barbrook Reservoir is a somewhat controversial water body to include in this book, but it has been included as an important case study in the management of wild-swimming spots. Little Barbrook, as it is called, is one of a series of small moorland reservoirs that were once managed and well-maintained, but which sadly are no longer. Around the turn of the century, the nearby Ramsay Reservoir **S1** was a popular roadside swim spot for Sheffielders, but the authorities drained it to prevent swimming. Now only a small volume of water remains there, enough to swim but not satisfactorily.

The upper Barbrook Reservoirs, once a large contiguous water body, is now a collection of pools that play host to a population of Canada geese, a large number of frogs, newts, lizards and other small creatures. While it is possible to swim in at least one of the pools, they are shallow and should probably be left to the wildlife. Which brings us to Little Barbrook: a small teardrop-shaped reservoir never more than about 2m deep; it is almost black due to the peat and is surrounded on three sides by raised ground, which means it receives the full thermal benefit of solar energy and little wind, warming it to unprecedented levels compared with the nearby River Derwent. Thankfully, it is over a kilometre away from the nearest road, along a 4x4 track, which keeps the number of visitors down, but during hot spells it quickly becomes one of the most popular Peak District swim spots. As a result, during most warm summers, signs are periodically erected and wardens patrol the area to discourage swimming to allow the place to breathe and recover. As with so many places that suffer the curse of social-media tagging, antisocial behaviour, littering, BBQs and fires are not uncommon but, thankfully, limited to hot spells. If you encounter rubbish, do take it away. If you encounter BBQs or fires,

INFORMATION

DISTANCE: 12.8km
TIME: 3–4 hours
MAP: OS Explorer OL24 The Peak District – White Peak Area
PARKING: Lay-bys on the A621 (SK 280 751; 53.2726, -1.5801)
PUBLIC TRANSPORT: Peakline 218 bus service from Sheffield to Baslow
SWIMMING: Silty swim at Ramsay **S1**, hidden pool by crossroads early in walk **S2**, sublime moorland reservoir at Barbrook **S3** towards end of walk
PLACES OF INTEREST: Ramsay Reservoir, White Edge, Barbrook Reservoirs
REFRESHMENTS: Occasionally a coffee van at Curbar Gap car park
VARIANTS: This route can be linked with any or all of the following walks for an epic trip: Walk 16 – Grindleford Derwent & Padley Gorge, Walk 17 – Froggatt Edge & Bridges, Walk 19 – Chatsworth

politely explain the associated risks. And if you find it is simply too busy, move on and find a secluded spot in the stream below the reservoir, which you won't be able to swim in, but you will have it all to yourself. Barbrook is an example of what is on the horizon if we are not able to secure access to more of our open water; the places we can access will be subject to greater pressures and thus greater management. If you arrive at the lay-bys and they are full, please go elsewhere; although you've made plans to visit a place, this does not mean that you can or should if others have arrived before you. If you arrived at a restaurant or the cinema to find it full, you would move on.

The walk starts and finishes at a pair of substantial lay-bys on the busy A621 between Sheffield and Baslow **1**. Head through the large white gate to check out Ramsay Reservoir first. Tucked largely out of sight behind a stand of trees, it is a pleasant stretch of water ringed by bright yellow gorse. Swim if you must **S1**, but there is a better spot close by that few know about. From Ramsay, retrace your steps a short distance **2** before dropping down to Fox Lane, a very quiet backroad with little traffic. Follow the road, keeping an eye out for a beautiful, cultivated stretch of blooming flowers on your left. Recross the A621 to a wooden gate on the other side; this leads to an indistinct path across the moors to Clodhall Lane **3**. When you reach the road, cross it to turn left and follow a faint path down to the river at the crossroads. It's admittedly noisy, thanks to the traffic, but it is a surprisingly deep, warm pool well worth a stop **S2**.

Pop back up the hill to the gate and recross Clodhall Lane to turn left and follow a delightful bouncy path across spongy moor to White Edge **4**; this is a relatively popular walker's path during the summer, but it has a remote and 'out there' feeling in a winter blizzard. Views from the Edge are fantastic. The full extent of Capability Brown's landscape design is evident at the Chatsworth House and Estate, which is laid out to the south, while Froggatt Edge, Stoney Middleton, Sir William Hill, Eyam and Bretton Moors and beyond to Stanage, Lose Hill and Win Hill lie to the north. Walking the length of the edge, some 4–5km, you will almost certainly see some of the wild herds of deer that roam on Big Moor to your right or down in the Serengeti-like yellow grassland between White Edge and Froggatt Edge to your left.

Arriving at a broken stone wall and wooden finger-post, we leave the Edge. Turn right along the wall **5**. There is a lovely rest/picnic spot on rounded rocks at the wall's end after 400m. From here turn left but be careful to take the right fork which brings you to the B6054. Follow this briefly, from the sanctuary of a path south of the road, to loop down to the collection of pools which once made Barbrook Reservoir. Sitting on the old dam wall above the pools watching the Canada geese and listening to the frogs makes for a good picnic spot. Continuing south, past the building which presumably once housed the managers of the reservoirs, the path turns into a 4x4 track and continues past old concrete holding tanks to Little Barbrook **S3**. If you are lucky, you will have the place to yourself. Most likely you won't, but once you are in the warm water there is plenty of space for all.

If you are in a hurry to get back to your car, simply follow the track to the gate. If you have a bit more time on your hands, identify the track in the heather adjacent to the dam wall and head up onto the moor to find a couple of stone circles. Barbrook I and II are some of the best examples of stone circles in the area, although the impressive looking Barbrook I, the first one you encounter, is thought to have been largely rebuilt by a farmer in 1989! From the second circle, drop down to the 4x4 track and turn left to return to the lay-by and your vehicle.

1 Park in one of the large lay-bys on either side of the main A621 Sheffield to Baslow road. Beware the high kerbs! Go through the big white gate on the E side of the road and follow the path S and then E to Ramsay Reservoir for a silty dip **S1**.

2 Backtrack 200m to a L turn which leads you to a quiet B road (Fox Lane). Turn R to walk along the road for 700m to the busy A621. Cross with care and go through the gate in the wall to follow the path across the moor via some low foot bridges to join Clodhall Lane.

3 Cross the road and follow the path SE, down the other side of the wall, to a delightful pool **S2** almost hidden from view by the bridge next to the A621. Retrace your steps to the road crossing point, recross it and head NW to reach White Edge trig point after 3km.

4 Continue NE for another 2.7km, along the well-trodden path along White Edge, to a broken wall and wooden fingerpost.

5 Turn R and follow the path along the S side of the wall to its end after 300m. Turn L, but take the R fork in a NE direction for 800m to the B6054.

6 Turn R and follow the path SE, which initially stays close to the S side of the wall on the S side of the road before it trends S to a collection of largely silted-up reservoirs after 1.2km. Explore or skirt around these to arrive at a gate and building after a further 600m.

7 Continue S past the building on a 4x4 track for 1km to Barbrook Reservoir **S3**.

8 Adjacent to the dam is a faint track up the steep heather-clad hill bounding the reservoir to the E. Take this and follow for 200m to a path. Turn R. Initially pass what looks like a stone circle on your R. Continue on to an actual stone circle after 400m.

9 The stone circle is set down below the path. Go past the circle and continue to join a 4x4 track which leads, after 400m, to the main road and your vehicle.

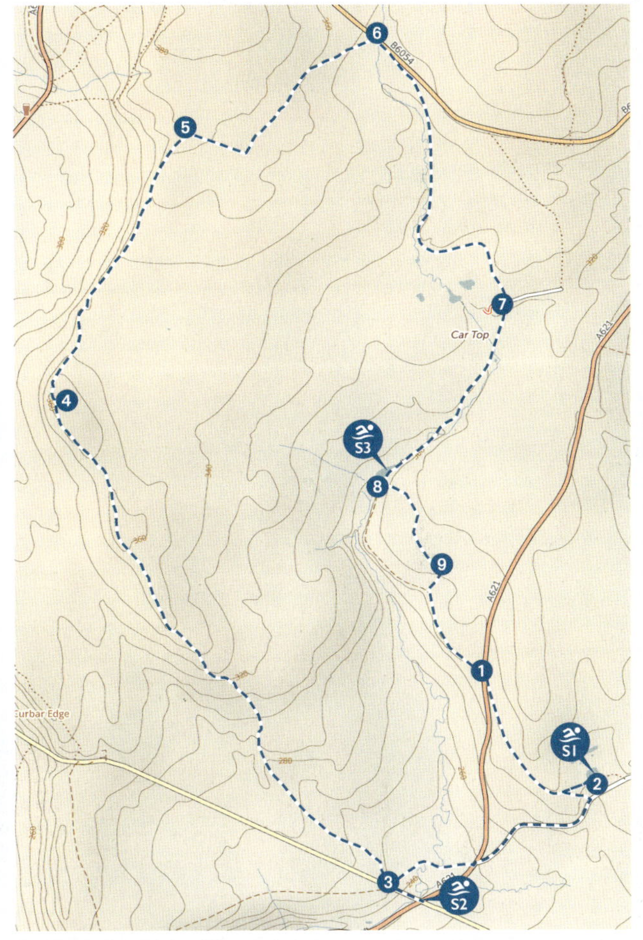

CHATSWORTH

Chatsworth Estate provides in abundance, from Capability Brown's immaculate landscaping and the majesty of the House itself to some fine swimming between two weirs.

The Chatsworth Estate is iconic, loved by both locals and visitors from afar, who appreciate the vision of the 18th-century landscape architect Capability Brown as much as the grandeur of one of the UK's favourite stately homes. The house sits on the bank of the River Derwent, and a walk through the grounds, past the outstandingly pretty Estate-owned village of Edensor, and a dip or two in the river are an essential addition to any book on swim-walks in the Peak District.

Commence at the car park of Calton Lees, next to the Chatsworth Garden Centre. The payment hut is open for much of the year: parking costs £5 and both cash and card are accepted. A small drinks and snacks kiosk opens on busy weekends, and there is a café/restaurant and loos in the garden centre. If you bring a dog with you, it must be on a lead for the entire walk. The paths pass through large areas of pastureland, home to sheep and deer, and the river is busy with ducks and herons. Swimming is not officially sanctioned by the estate, but it is widely accepted, with many gathering on hot summer's days to relax on the grassy banks and cool off in the water. Please respect this special place: pay for parking, take all litter home, use the loos in the garden centre or Edensor Tea Cottage and help to keep the place open and accessible.

Leave the car park on a tarmac track which passes the entrance to the garden centre ❶ and follows around to the right, through a gate, and uphill for approximately 1km to a series of bends by some holiday cottages ❷. After these cottages the route enters an experimental walled area that is being left to rewild. Whether the local deer population has an affinity for this 'wild' experience is unclear, but it is a worthy enterprise that may prove a headache for

INFORMATION

DISTANCE: 6.7km
TIME: 2 hours
MAP: OS Explorer OL24 The Peak District – White Peak Area
PARKING: Calton Lees pay & display car park (SK 258 686; 53.2140, -1.6144)
PUBLIC TRANSPORT: Bus service 218, operated by TM Travel, runs between Sheffield Interchange and Bakewell, stopping at Chatsworth daily
SWIMMING: Best between the two weirs **S1**
PLACES OF INTEREST: Chatsworth Garden Centre, Edensor, Chatsworth House
REFRESHMENTS: Chatsworth Garden Centre, Edensor Tea Cottage, kiosk at car park on busy weekends
VARIANTS: If time is short, you can walk up one side of the river and back down the other, omitting the 150m of ascent around to Edensor village, crossing the river at the bridge by Calton Lees and then the one up-river close to Chatsworth House

the estate management if it is successful enough to warrant expanding into the perfectly sculpted and manicured rolling deer fields framing the house. A final push up through the rewilding zone brings us into more traditional pastureland with peacefully grazing sheep. Cross the fields to a stand of trees. Before descending through the woods, look to your right and you will see the Russian Cottage. The cottage was inspired by a gift of a model of a Russian Farm to the Sixth Duke of Devonshire in 1855 from the brother of Tsar Nicholas of Russia. Following the duke's visit to Russia in 1816, when he served as the British Ambassador to the King, the tsar and the duke become friends. An exchange visit planned for 1844 was unable to go ahead, so the tsar sent an intricate model of a Russian farmhouse as a keepsake, which provided the inspiration to build the cottage.

Go through the gate and descend through the woods into the deer's domain. This is the realm of Lancelot Brown (born c. 1715–16), more commonly known as Capability Brown: an English gardener and landscape architect who remains the most famous figure in the history of the English landscape garden style. He designed more than 170 parks, many of which survive, with Chatsworth being one of the best examples. Criticism of his style mostly centres on the claim that he created 'identikit' landscapes, with the main house in a sea of turf, some water (albeit often an impressive feature) and trees in clumps and shelterbelts, showing a lack of imagination and even taste on the part of his patrons.

As you step out of the woods, through the impressively high wooden deer gate ❹, and look down onto his work, it is indeed impressive to see landscape gardening on such a scale, but it conflicts with its surroundings. Love it or hate it, it is certainly sensational.

Pass through his creation, between and below copses of mature trees. Neither he nor his employer who commissioned the work, the fourth Duke of Devonshire, lived to see them come to fruition. Being among the 300 fallow and 150 red deer as they graze among the trees is an exciting, almost magical, experience, but they are skittish and ever alert, liable to bolt en masse across the river, not unlike the migration of wildebeest across African plains!

Nestled below the trees is the estate village of Edensor (pronounced Endzor; population 145), a picture-postcard hamlet with an immaculate stone church, completely out of proportion to the number of houses, which served the family and guests of Chatsworth House. The history of the village is interesting, with successive dukes removing and rebuilding constituent parts to cater to their whims through the years, with a general purpose of housing many of the staff employed on the estate and in the house ❺. The Tea Cottage in Edensor is superb.

As you leave Edensor, a small climb on a gravel track remains before you finally drop down in front of the house itself, arriving at an attractive stone bridge over the River Derwent ❻. Here we turn right to follow the riverbank on the opposite side to the house. Swimming is possible in most of the river, but we recommend the stretch between the two weirs – it is possible to leave your stuff at the top weir and swim the entire 600m to the bottom one, and back again! Care should be taken getting in and out at the weirs, as the riverbed is rocky and the water dark with peat. When changing, please be mindful of the sensitivities of others, including non-swimmers, and behave politely. Now all that remains is a gentle 300m back uphill underneath a magnificent copper beech tree to the car park.

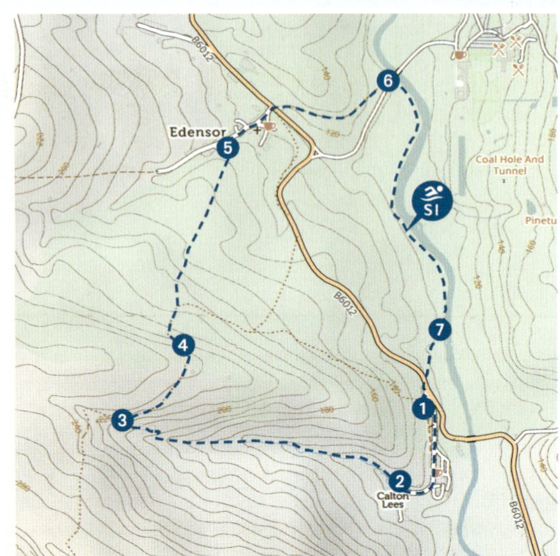

1 Leave the car park by walking away from its entrance/the road past the garden centre (last chance for a civilised loo stop for a few km). Keep R when passing the garden centre. Follow the tarmac road to the R to a fork. Go through the wooden gate to take the L fork (signposted 'Calton House & Calton Houses Cottage'). The road now turns from tarmac to gravel. (600m)

2 Follow the gravel track for 1.2km uphill to a pair of switchback bends at a cluster of cottages. Follow the switchbacks past the cottages into a short section of walled track to a wooden gate onto fields.

3 Go through the gate and turn R. Follow the track uphill to another gate after 200m. Go through the gate and into a larger field. Cross on the diagonal path to the woods on the far side, 200m away. Go through the gate and begin descending through the woods on a walled track to a massive 7-bar wooden (deer) gate.

4 Go through the gate to open pastureland. Look for the steep spire of the church at Edensor just poking out above the treetops; this is the reference point to aim for, but it will soon dip from sight below the treeline. Head downhill towards the spire (in the distance) and a large cluster of trees (foreground). Go through the trees and continue in the same direction on the far side. At the next stand of trees bear a little to the L to arrive at a quaint metal swing gate at the top of steep stone steps that lead into the centre of Edensor.

5 Turn R on the road through the village, passing the tearooms on the R just before reaching the main road. Cross the main road and continue along the gravel track as it rises a little before dropping down to the bridge over the River Derwent in front of Chatsworth House.

6 Turn R at the bridge, not crossing the river, to follow the bank. The first of two weirs is after 800m, the second after a further 600m. Swimming is possible all along the river, but it is best at and between the two weirs **SI**.

7 The car park lies 300m beyond the lower weir.

MONSAL HEAD

Quintessential English picnic spots lie hidden on the shaded, grassy banks of the River Wye.

Monsal Head is one of the prettiest and most popular beauty spots in the Peak District, a winning combination of spectacular views, the winding River Wye confined within a steep-sided dale, an historic viaduct, an excellent tourist trail and good facilities. You would be forgiven for wondering why we are recommending you visit such a tourist honeypot, but rest assured, the swimming is among the finest in the whole of the Peak District National Park and much of the walk is away from the multitudes.

We begin and end the walk at the popular viewpoint at Monsal Head. Park in the large 150-bay long-stay car park rather than the smaller short-stay parking at the overlook. Toilets and refreshments can be found in the Monsal Head Hotel and also at Hobb's Café. The Welsh poet W. H. Davies wrote the poem *Leisure*, which famously begins: '*What is this life if, full of care, we have no time to stand and stare.*' So stand for a while and admire the fine views up and down the dale.

In early October each year the area around the overlook becomes the focus of the road-cycling world as the Monsal Hill Climb takes place. First run in 1930, this event started out as a few mates riding out to Monsal Head at the end of the track-racing season and timing each other up the hill. At that time it was an unmade trail. It now attracts over 200 riders, ranging from club level to seasoned professionals.

We begin our walk by leaving the road at the overlook, on the apex of the top bend, and passing through a wooden gate **1** onto a narrow, gently descending pathway which drops down to the River Wye. Spare a sympathetic thought for the cyclists mentioned above, who accomplish this height gain in little over a minute. The present record, set in 1981, stands at 1 minute 14.1 seconds!

INFORMATION

DISTANCE: 7km
TIME: 2–3 hours
MAP: OS Explorer OL24 The Peak District – White Peak Area
PARKING: Monsal Head (SK 184 715; 53.2406, -1.7245)
PUBLIC TRANSPORT: 173 and 257 buses from Bakewell
SWIMMING: Lots of spots in the River Wye, downstream from the viaduct **S1** + **S2**
PLACES OF INTEREST: Monsal Head & viewpoint, Monsal Head Viaduct, Monsal Trail
REFRESHMENTS: Monsal Head Hotel, Hobb's Café
VARIANTS: When you arrive at the Monsal Trail late in the walk, it is worth a there-and-back route of a few hundred metres to the SE to look down from the Monsal Viaduct. If you have time, it is also worth walking a few kilometres in the other direction towards Water-cum-Jolly Dale for more outstanding vistas

Your arrival at the river is heralded by the low rumble of falling water as a graceful semi-circular weir, constructed in Victorian times, cascades over a series of steps. Fencing and signage discourage access from this bank, but a short way downstream is a footbridge ❷ into an expansive, wild meadow bordering the riverbank. Crossing the bridge and turning right gives access to the river downstream of the weir, with many paddling opportunities. The river widens, with easy beach access to deeper water and our first swim spot ⑤①. Picnickers will almost certainly be in the meadow by lunchtime, so an early start will avoid them.

From the meadow, head downstream along the obvious footpath. The path is mainly set away from the side of the river, but smaller subsidiary paths follow the bank for most of the way. These lesser paths lead to a series of secluded spots that rival any other swimming in the whole of the Peak District. The best is found quite early on ⑤②, around 300m from the large meadow and bridge. A large tree

overhangs a pool and waterfall in the river, with a picnicking area abundant with wild flowers. There are more spots over the next kilometre, maybe not quite as beautiful as the first, but well worth seeking out.

After 1.5km a large wooden signpost indicates the point at which we leave the river ❸ and head steeply uphill into the woods. Most visitors stay by the river, so the shaded woods may feel both quieter and cooler. The path zigzags uphill for a while before breaking back out of the woods onto a farm track ❹. Follow this track to and through the farm, paying attention to the signs. Beyond the farm the lane continues, with fine views of Monsal Head and beyond, before dropping back down ❺ into the woods and descending to the Monsal Trail.

The Monsal Trail is a traffic-free route for walkers, cyclists, horse riders and wheelchair users through some of the Peak District's most spectacular limestone dales. It runs along the former Midland Railway line for 14km, between Blackwell Mill in Chee Dale and Coombs Road in Bakewell. The public can now experience the full length of the former railway route at their own pace and enjoy breathtaking views at places like Water-cum-Jolly Dale (just a few km northwest), which had remained hidden since the railway closed in 1968. Our route meets the trail just a few hundred metres from the Monsal Viaduct (southeast), where huge arches support the route over the deep depths of the dale. From the intersection, take the steep footpath due south down to a large meadow beneath the viaduct. Walk under the arches and marvel at Victorian engineering before arriving at a pretty footbridge over the river. Turn right to follow a fairly steep path back to the Monsal Head and a well-deserved ice cream and drink.

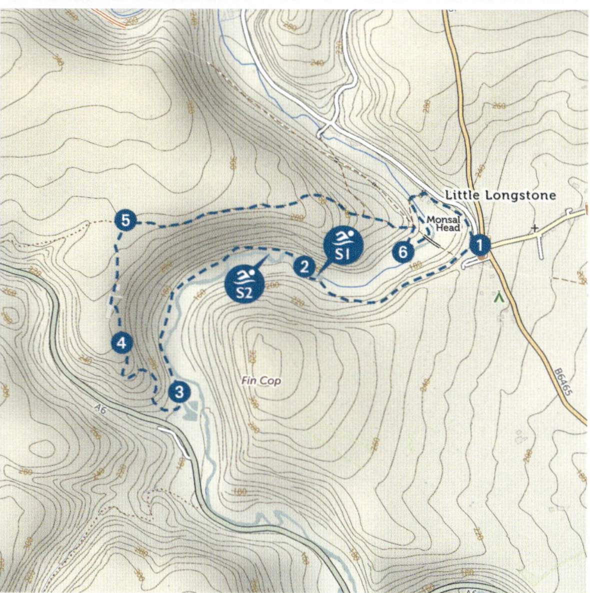

1 Park in the large pay & display long-stay car park adjacent to the Monsal Head Hotel, not the short-stay car park at the overlook. Turn L, immediately downhill, at the top hairpin bend next to Hobb's Café. Follow the narrow and gently sloping path down through the woods for 800m to an impressive weir on the River Wye.

2 Cross the river on the footbridge to a large meadow with multiple opportunities to swim **S1**. From here follow the path downstream, on the N bank, for 1.5km past many more swim spots, the best of which is just 300m from the bridge by a large tree overhanging a pool and waterfall **S2**.

3 At a large wooden signpost (White Lodge one way, Monsal Head the other), turn R to head uphill into the woods. Continue as the path makes a large zigzag through the woods before arriving at a track to a farm. (600m)

4 Continue along the track, following the home-made signs directing you through the the farm (sometimes cows around). At 100m after leaving the farm go through a gate in a stone wall. Bear R across the field to a signpost at its far edge.

5 The signpost is on the edge of Brushfield Lane, a well-used farm track. Follow this for 1.5km to the Monsal Trail, a well-maintained bridleway between Bakewell and Buxton. Turn R to follow a steep path down to the River Wye.

6 Turn L to follow the path upstream to pass underneath the Monsal viaduct. Follow the riverside path upstream for 200m to a picturesque bridge. Cross this, turn R and follow the path back to the Monsal Head Hotel and your start point 400m from the bridge.

YOULGREAVE & LATHKILL DALE

Loop through Lathkill Dale with its crystal-clear waters, swim in the village lido at Youlgreave and keep your eyes peeled for water vole colonies in the River Bradford.

The Bradford and Lathkill rivers are among the clearest (and coldest!) in the Peak District. Both are quiet, shallow streams, with little in the way of waterfalls or cataracts, as opposed to fully-fledged rivers. As a result, their tranquil natures have resulted in their nominations as designated nature conservation areas hosting an abundance of verdant vegetation, a wide variety of birdlife and rare, protected populations of water voles. This is a walk to be taken at a slow pace, matching the rivers' flow, soaking up the history and bathing in nature as much as the water.

We begin in the sleepy hamlet of Alport ❶, a tiny scattering of old stone-built houses, many with riverside gardens worthy of inclusion in lifestyle and travel magazines. 'Hidden gems in the crown of a regal landscape' is how Victorian travel writer James Croston described the Derbyshire villages of Rowsley, Nether Haddon and Alport over a hundred years ago. Built as a result of lead extraction, Alport was once a bustling industrial area underpinned by a lattice of mine workings. A sign immediately as one leaves Alport gives some detailed information and sets the tone for the protected nature of the area ❷. Although much of the water appears enticing, it's not all accessible for swimming. If you're patient and lucky enough, you may see evidence of water vole colonies, one of the UK's most rapidly declining mammals. Folk walk these banks with their dogs, but signage clearly explains why much of the water is out of bounds for our canine friends, largely due to the problem of pollution from flea treatments washing into the water. Please do read the signs and respect their purpose.

As you follow the south bank of the Bradford, there is evidence of the area's industrial past, but you'd be forgiven for not noticing. Mine entrances in the limestone outcrops are concealed by

rampant greenery, and wildflower meadows carpet the collapsed chambers beneath as nature reclaims its former glory. Rock climbers may sometimes be seen on the limestone faces, and the electric-blue flash of kingfishers darting above the clear waters accentuates the air of peace and tranquillity that pervades this most special area. There is a palpable feeling of history having unfolded here.

Early in the walk, after around 1km **3**. the larger village of Youlgreave hosts one of the finest examples of community space in the Peak District. Despite the rules and regulations imposed by the conservation area, the village has built and maintains a natural lido or swimming pool **S1** as part of the Bradford. Essentially a widening in the river, it has been dammed to create a pool just over a metre deep. With an expansive meadow sloping to its bank, and just a stone's throw from the village, the pool plays host to locals and visitors alike when they want to cool off on a hot day. This is the only true swimming spot on the whole walk, most of the rest being shallow paddling pools, so make the most of it. At the road crossing just before the lido our route joins the Limestone Way, an impressive 74km waymarked route across the White Peak landscape of the Peak District National Park. We follow it for 3km, so look out for the signposts with a ram's head logo.

From the lido follow the Bradford upstream past a series of impressive ponds excavated during the mining heyday, now largely reclaimed by nature, with only the dams and occasional piece of ironmongery hinting at their provenance. The water is calm and silent, with potential for some careful immersion. If the lido was too busy for your liking, then picnic spots abound along this stretch, which will likely be much quieter **S2**.

Our walk now switches watersheds, from the Bradford to the Lathkill **4**. A steep climb through deeply shaded woodland with overtones of The Lost World brings us into upland fields bounded by blue-grey limestone walls. Stiles and gates pick a way through the labyrinth. In May, carpets of bright yellow dandelions and buttercups make a bold colour change to the deep greens of the wild garlic and giant ferns below. A fine country house on your left enjoys panoramic views towards Matlock to your right. Follow the Limestone Way ram's head plaques for a few hundred metres beyond the house and head due north across a patchwork of fields bounded by a plethora of stone walls. If distance is your priority for the day, it is possible to add about 6km by continuing along the Limestone Way to enter Lathkill Dale further upstream.

At **6**, the edge of the escarpment, enjoy the last expansive views before dropping back into the different world of water and greenery that is Lathkill Dale. A low footbridge crosses the quiet stream next to a quiet road **S3**, with paddling possible upstream. Although our route turns right here to follow the watercourse downstream, a lung-busting walk up the hill will bring you into the picturesque village of Over Haddon, with refreshments. And toilets!

Lathkill Dale is really special, but largely confined within a nature reserve so please respect the signs. The flow of the stream is slowed to what feels like a complete standstill, as the water has been shaped, over the years, into a continuous series of pools, each feeding into the next via a small step, forming busy little waterfalls. The water is crystal clear, with myriad flora and fauna. The banks remain largely unspoilt by the picnickers who settle in for the afternoon, thanks to the informative signposting.

We now follow the footpath alongside the stream as far as a tarmac road **7**, which we follow for the last stretch back into Alport.

1 Park in one of the generous lay-bys on either side of the road (Alport Lane). Walk due E along the road for 100m to a R turn along the river Bradford. Follow this for another 100m to a large white, wooden gate.

2 Go through the gate and follow a well-graded track alongside the river, past limestone outcrops on your L, through an open meadow. Go through a wooden swing gate after 300m. Continue to a beautiful stone bridge on your R after a further 300m. Ignore the bridge and continue for a further 200m, bending R to a road crossing on the outskirts of Youlgreave.

3 Cross the road and continue, through a wooden gate with a rules and regulations sign for Youlgreave Conservation Area, for 300m to Youlgreave Lido **S1**. Continue in the same direction along the Bradford to a shallow paddling spot next to a low concrete footbridge after 200m **S2**. Keep on along the S bank past a beautiful series of shallow pools with grassy picnic areas **S3** at around 400m. After following the river for a further 500m you will arrive at a stone bridge.

4 Cross the bridge and follow the Limestone Way steeply uphill through shady woodland for 500m

to a quiet tarmac road (Weaddow Lane). Turn R and follow the road for 400m, past open panoramas on your R and a country house on your L, to a footpath on your L.

5 Turn L on the Limestone Way footpath on a sharp bend in the road. Climb uphill through an open field for 100m to another road crossing (Coldwell End). Continue due N for another 400m, through open fields with stone walls, stiles and gates, to cross Moor Lane (more of a track than a road). A further 300m in a NW direction, through more fields and a stand of trees, brings you to Back Lane. A final 1km in a NNE direction over yet more fields and stiles, through a working farm, brings you to the edge of a tree-lined edge above Lathkill Dale.

6 Bear E and then W on a good track down through the woods to reach the river after 500m. There is a paddling spot by the footbridge **S4**. Continue E along the N bank of the Lathkill. Pass shallow verdant paddling spots after 200m before entering the Lathkill Nature Reserve (no swimming) and idyllic riverside picnic spots after a further 500m. At 300m beyond the picnic spots is a tarmac road.

7 Cross the river on the road and follow it for 150m before turning L on a footpath. A further 1.3km of well-trodden footpaths, through gates, but mostly away from the river, brings you back into Alport and your transport.

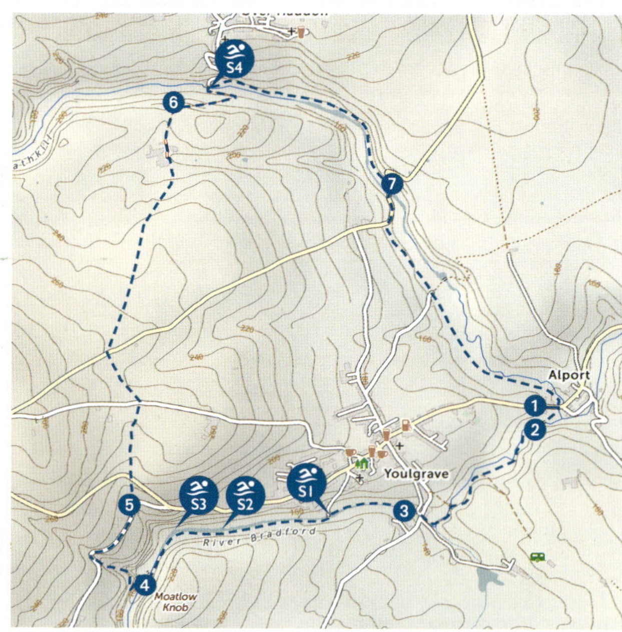

LIMESTONE
WAY

MATLOCK SWOOSH

This very pleasant walk explores the outskirts of Matlock and finishes with a kilometre of floating down the River Derwent with the slow-moving current.

'swoosh' is usually a section of river subject to an ebbing tide that funnels water through at a much faster rate than elsewhere. With there being no tidal rivers in the Peak District, we choose stretches of rivers that are deep enough to swim in, with enough flow to swoosh you along. A stretch of the Derwent immediately north of Matlock has just such a swoosh. Before you raise your expectations too high, this is no adrenaline ride, but more of a gentle float through very pretty countryside. In other parts of the world somebody would be renting inner tubes and selling cold beers to intrepid backpackers to float beneath a tropical canopy full of swinging monkeys. Alas, it's the UK and unless you're accustomed to immersing yourself in fairly chilly water for half an hour, you're going to choose to substitute the rubber of the inner tube for the neoprene of a wetsuit. Pack whatever you choose to swim in into a waterproof dry bag, so you can put your walking clothes and footwear into the bag for the river section.

The walk begins from a small lay-by at the side of the busy A6 as it enters Matlock from the north **1**. Head southeast along the railway line to cross the Derwent on a Victorian metal footbridge. Look down at the river and remember this spot, as it will be the point at which you exit the swoosh at the end of the walk. Turn back on yourself to now follow the river upstream, past an abandoned factory on your left, to open farmland **2**. The walk traces a route along footpaths through fields to gentle hills, verdant woodland **3** and a rather pleasant open but hidden valley **4**. The name Matlock translates as 'moot oak' or an oak tree where meetings were held. It's easy to see how the name came about, as these majestic trees dot the fields.

INFORMATION

DISTANCE: 11km
TIME: 3 hours
MAP: OS Explorer OL24 The Peak District – White Peak Area
PARKING: Small car park opposite Premier Inn on the A6 north of Matlock (SK 287 609; 53.1445, -1.5718)
PUBLIC TRANSPORT: 172 bus between Bakewell and Matlock
SWIMMING: Half an hour of floating down the River Derwent at the end of the walk **S1**
PLACES OF INTEREST: Turkey Dip Rocks, Matlock Swoosh
REFRESHMENTS: Square & Compass, Three Stags Heads
VARIANTS: If you prefer not to carry your swimming kit, it's not far to walk back to the car, change into your swim gear and head back to the entry stone, but that would rather defeat the purpose of a swim-walk. It is also possible to get into the water by the Three Stags Head to extend the river-swim element of the walk

A short climb brings you to the high point of the walk and an impressive holiday cottage built into the hillside with dramatic views across the Derwent flood plain ❺. Bunker-like, this would be a great place in which to hunker down and watch a storm. Now head steeply downhill through woodland to another valley, this one carpeted with thick grasses and willow herb.

Although there are two very small water bodies in these woods, neither are suitable for swimming, so be patient. At the second of the two ponds (out of sight of the path but identified by the 'No Swimming' sign on a tree) is a cave worth seeking out. Used by rock climbers, it's known as Turkey Dip Rocks and overlooks the pond ❻. If you're unlucky enough to get caught in the rain, this handy picnic spot stays completely dry.

The route now passes through the small village of Darley Bridge, home to the Three Stags Heads pub if you need refreshments or a loo stop before getting into the water. Immediately after the pub, the route heads back onto more open fields, past grazing cows, to join and then follow the Derwent ❼. Keep close to the riverbank and look out for a distinctive stone lying between the path and the river; it looks like an old gritstone gatepost on its side. Immediately next to it is a path down to a beach on a bend in the river; this is your entry point. Get changed on the beach, pop your walking clothes and footwear into your dry bag and wade in. It is soon deep enough to lie on your back and float feet first down the river. If you encounter any fishermen, engage with them politely. They may be quite happy for you to float quietly by, or they may prefer you to exit, walk downriver and re-enter below them (this may be tricky as much of the bank is fairly heavily vegetated, but should still be possible). Beware of fallen trees and submerged branches. Don't enter the river if it's in any state of

flood (if the beach by the stone is submerged, this is probably a good indicator that the flow will be too fast).

After a kilometre of peaceful floating beneath a broken canopy and alongside dippers and herons, you will start to see signs of civilisation, as the river is sandwiched between the outskirts of the town and long-abandoned industry. Your exit point is on the left (north) bank below the footbridge you crossed at the start of the walk. Climb the steep, rocky bank, regaining your land legs, and follow the narrow footpath alongside the railway line back to your car. The float takes around 30 lazy minutes, somewhat faster if swim-assisted.

1 Park in the small lay-by (room for about 10 vehicles) opposite the Premier Inn on the A6 on the N edge of Matlock. Cross the railway line to the S and turn immediately L to follow a narrow path alongside the tracks, over the River Derwent (500m). As soon as you have crossed the river, turn immediately R to leave the railway line and follow a footpath between the river and a dilapidated, disused factory on your L for 800m to open fields. (1.3km in total)

2 Head W across the middle of the field, away from the river, for 200m to a stile onto a quiet road. Turn R on the road and follow for 150m to turn due S on a footpath at a wooden fingerpost. Follow the path for a further 300m through one field and then another to a wall with a very wide metal gate set in it. (650m total)

3 Bear R on a footpath through fields of grazing cows towards a hillside. Follow the path up the lower slopes of the hillside to a wooden stile in a wall after 700m. Cross this and continue along the top boundary of another field to a stone pinch-gate. Continue past a stone barn/building with a rusty corrugated-iron roof on your R. Continue through a five-bar wooden gate along a walled track to a narrow valley. (1.4km in total)

4 Walk up the valley for 700m, passing through a wooden gate next to a metal one before arriving at a gravel track and wooden fingerpost. Bear L along the track, past a large log store and house on the R. The path climbs up to a tarmac road on the edge of a small hamlet after 300m. Turn R along the road before crossing it and turn L on a footpath after

30m or so. Follow the R edge of a field uphill to an unusual holiday cottage with fine views, built into the ground. (1.6km in total)

5 Continue N past the cottage and along the fence, keeping L at the trees. Head downhill into the woods over another wooden stile and steps to a pond – sadly, not swimmable despite the life ring. (300m) Continue for a further 300m downhill through the woods to arrive at a gravel track. Turn R and follow it uphill to a kind of T-junction after about 50m. Bear R immediately before the track turns L at a barbed-wire fence. (700m total)

6 Follow the path alongside the fence, initially along a grassy-bottomed, wooded valley, for 700m to a small bridge over a stream. Continue following the

valley/stream. After a further 600m there is a 'No Swimming' sign on a tree at a junction. Turn R here to have a look at the impressive cave above another stagnant pool before returning to the route. Another 300m brings you to a tarmac road and into the small village of Darley Bridge.

7 Turn R and follow the pavement through the village past the Three Stags Heads pub, bearing L at the T-junction to cross the River Derwent again after 200m. After another 50m turn R past Flatts Farm. Follow a path due E through fields for 600m to meet the river again. Bear R to follow the riverside footpath for 800m to a distinctive stone which looks like an old gatepost lying on its side. (1650m in total)

8 This marks the entry point for the swim section of the walk, a 1km 'swoosh' down the Derwent **S1**. Enter the river and go with the flow until underneath the footbridge you crossed at the very start of the walk. For the most part it is deep enough to swim, with a gentle current. Exit on the L (N) shore. Scramble up the steep, rocky bank under the bridge to the footpath by the railway line. Turn L and follow it 500m back to the car.

LUMSDALE FALLS & MATLOCK

Explore the fascinating mill town of Matlock on foot, showering and swimming at the archaeologically important Lumsdale Falls before returning over High Tor.

Lumsdale Falls is a hidden surprise. An old mill in the heart of Matlock is not the first place a wild swimmer would expect to take a dip but combined with a walk over High Tor and a section of the Derwent, it presents a great urban swim-walk steeped in history. Firstly, a caveat: Lumsdale Valley is an archaeological site; it is fenced off and privately managed. The gates are left open to the public between 1 May and 1 October but are closed outside of those months, so this is not a walk to do in the winter.

The walk starts in the centre of Matlock at a large pay & display car park between the A6 and the River Derwent, just south of the large Sainsbury's ❶. Note that the car park has a 2m-height barrier so no high-top vans. From the car park head north on the pavement along the busy A6, back towards Sainsbury's. Follow the footpath for just a short distance to an impressive metal footbridge over the Derwent on your right. You may see kayakers whooshing along below the bridge as the river is fast flowing; downriver a dedicated white-water section with slalom gates is used by an active local kayak club and others. Once over the bridge turn left and follow the Derwent up-river, past picnic benches and tables and a good number of access points to the river, some via steps. Swimming is possible here ⓢⓘ, but be aware that the water is fast flowing, especially after rain.

The path continues along the river before bending to the right to the well-manicured Knowleston Gardens ❷ and then past Hall Leys Park, a public park right in the centre of Matlock. Continue through the park, past playgrounds and a toddler's water park, before following a narrow-gauge railway on your right. The

INFORMATION

DISTANCE: 7.4km
TIME: 2–3 hours
MAP: OS Explorer OL24 The Peak District – White Peak Area
PARKING: Large pay & display car park alongside the A6 just south of Sainsbury's (SK 296 594; 53.1316, -1.5581)
PUBLIC TRANSPORT: Matlock lies on bus routes from Buxton, Sheffield & Chesterfield
SWIMMING: Below Lumsdale Falls is a smaller waterfall ⓢ②, Lumsdale Falls ⓢ③, River Derwent ⓢⓘ
PLACES OF INTEREST: Matlock, Lumsdale Falls & Mill, High Tor, Heights Of Abraham, River Derwent
REFRESHMENTS: Countless cafés, pubs and restaurants. We liked Bentley Brook Brewery & Taproom and Derwent Treescapes
VARIANTS: From point 2, if you have youngsters, they may enjoy a visit to the attractive and well-maintained Hall Leys Park which has a water park, model railway and picnic benches

route passes plaques commemorating the life of a policeman, who died after successfully rescuing a drowning person in 1911, and also the scarily impressive high-water marks that record the flood levels reached in the 1960s. Follow the directions through a residential area to cross the main road as it heads south out of Matlock, before following Butts Drive; this pleasant, narrow stone path on the edge of woodland leads to Bentley Brook ❸.

The stream has shallow pools pleasant for toddlers to splash about in, but none deep enough for swimming. However, on the far bank of the stream an outflow from a minor tributary creates a gushing waterfall perfect for a natural power shower! After your shower follow the road uphill past Bentley Brook Brewery & Taproom, a nice spot to rest up and enjoy a drink and piece of cake. Beyond the brewery a very old footpath on your left climbs steeply through the wood to the Wishing Stone ❹, a large natural gritstone rock, about 14ft in diameter. In times gone by some believed that to be granted a wish you had to run round the outer ring of the stone nine times. The number of

circuits needed varies in different sources, but some output of energy was needed if a wish was to be granted! Sadly, the perimeter of the stone is now a little overgrown. Rest awhile atop the stone before descending back through the woods on a different path in the direction of Lumsdale Falls/Mill.

Assuming that the gates are open ❺, it's a fairly obvious route through the site, with metal railings and signage indicating where you can and can't go. Thankfully, it is possible to scramble down to the water itself below the main drop of the falls, where you can once again power shower under the impressive waterfall. A great small cave on the far bank affords a very moody view of the water if you can cross over. Designated a scheduled ancient monument because of its historic importance, the Lumsdale Valley was once a bustling centre of industry, with a collection of mills powered by water from Bentley Brook. The brook, which rises on Matlock Moor, has never been known to dry up and supplies Lumsdale Falls with a constant water supply. The area was used for industrial purposes from the 17th century to the height of its production in the mid-19th century. Some mills were used for cotton spinning and bleaching, and some for grinding corn, bone and minerals. The site was used until the 1930s and is now one of the best examples of a water-powered industrial archaeological site in Britain, unique in its extensive use of water power in such a small area. The ruins of six of the mills in the Lumsdale Valley remain, all in various states of disrepair. The last private owner of the site refused to sell the buildings, despite lucrative offers for the stone, preferring to keep them in their ruinous state as a testament to their heritage and as a habitat for wildlife. The site is now owned by the Arkwright Society, a charity devoted to the rescue of industrial heritage buildings, hence the need to respect the fences, signage and general character of the place.

When you have had your fill of showering, ruin scrambling and info-board reading, the walk retraces the route past Bentley Brook Mill for about a kilometre before crossing a main road ❻ to climb above the town, giving good views of the unique geography of the River Derwent and the steep-sided valleys with tumbling brooks, which led to its industrial role. We then enter yet another well-maintained park, clearly a hallmark of the local council, who recognise the importance of public

space. High Tor Park plays host to the magnificent limestone cliffs of High Tor and Pic Tor ❼. Our route keeps its altitude to traverse along the top of the cliffs, with dizzying views down to the Derwent below and across to the Heights Of Abraham, an unusual cable car more commonly seen in the European Alps. Take heed of the signs indicating precipitous edges as the path winds its way past the haunts of rock climbers before dropping majestically back down into Matlock, past Pic Tor ❽, to the metal footbridge you crossed at the beginning of the walk.

1 Park in the large pay & display car park alongside the A6 adjacent to Matlock centre, just S of the large Sainsbury's. From the N end of the car park turn R to follow the pavement N back towards Matlock centre for 100m until a footbridge on the R crosses the River Derwent. Once over the bridge turn L to follow a wide track through trees alongside the river for 400m, past picnic tables and benches and potential swim spots **S1** (if you are happy in fast-flowing water), as it bends around to the R to Knowleston Gardens.

2 Continue on the path, ignoring the wooden footbridge on your L, through a black wrought-iron swing gate onto Stoney Way. Turn L to cross a bridge and turn immediately R on Knowleston Place. Follow this to the main road (Matlock Green). Turn R and follow the road for 300m to turn L on Butts Drive. Immediately, take the R fork on the public footpath.

3 Follow the narrow footpath for 1km to a bridge over a river (Bentley Brook) immediately before Lumsdale Road. Just a few metres before the bridge and the road follow a path into the woods on your L along the L bank of the river. After 200m the path runs out at some stepping stones. Cross these. On the opposite bank is a waterfall issuing from a culvert underneath Lumsdale Road **S2**. Climb up to Lumsdale Road and turn L to follow it gently uphill for 400m past Bentley Brook Brewery & Taproom to a footpath on the L.

4 Follow the footpath steeply uphill to the Wishing Stone. From the stone turn R to follow a steep footpath back down through the woods to rejoin Lumsdale Road. Turn R and follow the road downhill for around 60m to a L fork. Turn L and follow for 100m to a gate on your R to Lumsdale Fall Mill.

5 If the gates are open, go through them to follow the path through the private site, past the amazing Lumsdale Mill and waterfalls **S3**. If the site is closed, return to Lumsdale Road and turn L. Either way follow Lumsdale Road back down past the brewery for 1km, as far as Alfreton Road.

6 Cross the busy road with care and dogleg up a minor access road, past Derwent Treescapes (on your L). Follow the road which turns into a footpath, taking the R fork after 200m, and the L fork just after a wooden stile after a further 600m before arriving at a pretty terrace of houses after a further 300m. Here join Riber Road and follow it R, downhill around a sharp, steep corner to join Starkholmes Road. Follow this for 200m to High Tor Road on your L.

7 Follow High Tor Road for 400m, keeping R after 100m, until you arrive at a sharp R-hand bend in the tarmac track. On the bend continue straight on for 30m to join a footpath which roughly follows the edge of the cliffs. Turn R to follow it for 700m, past viewpoints over the valley below, always keeping L but being well aware of the steep drops if you go too far L! At Artist's Corner, bear R to descend for 500m, past horse paddocks on your R and with a view of Matlock before you, to the W end of Pic Tor Lane.

8 Turn L to follow the steep footpath down underneath the old railway line, as far as the River Derwent. Cross the bridge and turn L at the road to return to the car park.

DOVE DALE & ILAM ROCK

Dove Dale is known locally for the Dovedale Dash, the River Dove and Ilam Rock, as well as for its impressive limestone ravines, but the most iconic part of a trip to Dove Dale for many is the picturesque stepping stones.

The first Dovedale Dash took place on the Bonfire Party Weekend at Ilam Hall Youth Hostel in 1953 as a challenge between the cyclists and the walkers of the Derby Mercury Running Club. It was intended to run off the excesses of the party, and in the first race there were about 15 entrants. It now attracts over 1,000 runners, who sprint from Thorpe Farm down to the stepping stones, where the majority wade through the river in a frenzy of white water, before looping around towards Ilam Hall and back for a recrossing of the Dove and a steep uphill finish. If you don't happen to be here on the first Sunday of October, then this local tradition will likely pass you by, but when you are on the stepping stones stop, look up the hill and try to picture 1,000 runners descending at lightning speed towards you. It's quite some spectacle!

The walk starts from the well-proportioned National Trust pay & display Dove Dale car park ❶. Follow the wheelchair-friendly track out of the north corner of the car park for 500m, alongside the gently flowing, shallow Dove to the Stepping Stones ❷. There is no alternative but to cross the stones or wade the river; the gated path on the south bank of the river is on private land. At busy times queues form at the stones so an early start is advisable. If you are comfortable doing so, stop midway across to examine the limestone stones, which are pockmarked with a multitude of tiny fossils. It is likely that at this point in the walk you won't feel warm enough to swim, so we recommend

INFORMATION

DISTANCE: 8km
TIME: 3–4 hours
MAP: OS Explorer OL24 The Peak District – White Peak Area
PARKING: Dove Dale pay & display car park (SK 146 509; 53.0556, -1.7833)
PUBLIC TRANSPORT: Moorlands Connect on-demand bus service (Moorlandsconnect.co.uk)
SWIMMING: Plenty of waist-to-chest-deep spots along the River Dove. The best spots are marked **S1** – **S4**
PLACES OF INTEREST: Dove Dale Stepping Stones, Thorpe Hill, Ilam Rock
REFRESHMENTS: None
VARIANTS: We suggest a quick detour up Thorpe Hill early in the walk to warm you up ready for some swimming. Once you have crossed the stepping stones, follow the blue-topped waymarking signs in a spiral clockwise direction up to the summit for some impressive views. Retrace your steps to the route. This detour adds a total of 2km there and back and 140m of height gain and descent

a short detour up the adjacent Thorpe Hill. The footpath to the pointed summit begins immediately on the right after the stepping stones. It is waymarked with blue-topped wooden posts; please avoid the many subsidiary paths which have contributed much erosion to the faces. The advantage of the marked path is a gradual spiral route that gains the summit with only one short stretch of slippery, steep ground near the top, best avoided in the wet if you are uneasy with heights. The view from the ridge-like summit is splendid in every direction. Follow the same path back down to the stepping stones. After 2km and 140m of height gain and descent, you will probably welcome a swim.

There is a fine spot 500m up-river from the stepping stones **S1**, where the river deepens to about 1.5m. The water is cool, as is usually the case in the Peak District's limestone dales, but refreshing. A short distance further on, the path diverges from the river temporarily to climb a long series of shallow steps **3**. Towards the top of these steps is a faint path off to the left leading steeply down a slippery defile to the river. While it is not deep enough to properly swim here, there is a delightful grassy picnic spot and the water is good for paddling. Due to the precipitous nature of the path, it is unlikely many others will be there **S2**.

Once you've descended the steps on the other side, you are back by the river, initially on a path and then on a narrow wooden boardwalk. All along the route are steep-sided limestone walls and buttresses. These are interspersed in places by small caves and two plaques commemorating F. A. Holmes and W. Holmes, who championed the dale and its surrounding land as National Trust property throughout much of the 20th century. At 500m from the steps the path again diverges from the river. By the river's edge, is an idyllic picnic and bathing spot with relatively fast-flowing water whipping long manes of vivid green waterweed in its flow (**4** and **S3**). Continuing for a further 800m brings us to the lofty Ilam Rock, an unlikely-looking leaning monolith of limestone, a prize attraction for elite rock climbers. Beneath the pinnacle is a footbridge with further swimming potential (**5** and **S4**).

Cross the bridge and turn right to continue up-river for just a few hundred metres before the path turns left uphill. The climb is very steep and rocky, with many steps, quite a contrast with the route thus far. The exertion of the climb is somewhat compensated by its beauty as you pass through groves of wild garlic, bluebells and vivid purple corncockles, in the shade of mighty beech and sycamore trees. Upon arriving at the rim of the dale, the path turns left to hug the edge as it passes through Dove Dale Wood. On the edge of the wood is a working farm, which necessitates careful observation of the signs to avoid private land and circuit around to its west. You may encounter a particularly aggressive but seemingly harmless little terrier, which guards the wooden gate in a troll-like manner **6**.

Beyond the farm the route traverses the flanks of the delightfully named Bunster Hill, surely the inspiration for some Enid Blyton novels, below an ancient burial mound and above a pair of natural springs, to emerge onto a vertiginous spot overlooking Thorpe Hill in the distance. We drop off the ridge to follow a straightforward footpath past another farm to return to the car park. There are no refreshments available on the walk, so a visit to Ilam Country Park, just a kilometre away in Ilam, may be called for.

1 Walk NE out of the car park, past an information board and map, along a flat, wide, paved track alongside the River Dove, with the river on your R. Continue for 600m to a set of stepping stones across the river.

2 Cross the stepping stones and turn L to continue up the river. Good swim spot after 500m **S1**. Continue another 200m to a long series of shallow steps.

3 Climb these steps for 100m to a faint path on your L down to the river. It is steep and slippery but has a quiet grassy area by the water with dipping, not swimming, potential. Nice for a picnic away from the crowds on the main path **S2**.

4 Continue for 500m to where the path diverges from the river. Here follow the riverbank to a nice picnic spot with more opportunity for a swim **S3**. Continue for a further 800m on a narrow boardwalk, past caves and a National Trust plaque, to a footbridge below the impressive Ilam Rock. Swimming is pleasant near the bridge **S4**.

5 Cross the bridge and follow the river up on the opposite bank for 200m to a L turn into the woods. Climb very steeply up steps and rocks to reach the edge of the escarpment (100m of height gain over 300m covered!). The path then levels out and begins the return journey back along the rim of the valley, through a beech wood, to a farm after 1.1km

6 Pay attention to the signposts near the farm before heading due W along a farm track. Follow this for 200m before turning due S alongside a wall and a line of trees. After a further 200m bear R at a fork, through a gap in a wall, ignoring the sign straight on to Bunster Hill, instead skirting underneath its flank. Follow the path first through a field and then alongside a wall on your R for 500m downhill to a crossroads. Turn L to follow a narrow single track which contours across the hill to crest a ridge overlooking Thorpe Hill.

7 Descend from the ridge in the direction of Thorpe Hill (SE), to cross fields to a farm just above the car park. (900m)

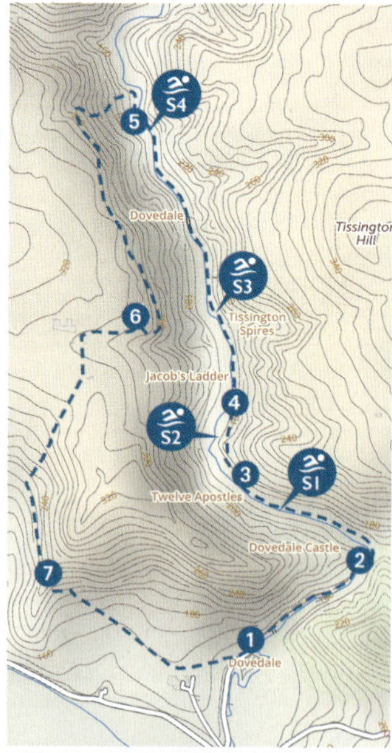

PIKE POOL

A pleasantly easy outing through Beresford Dale, past the impressive Pike Pool to bridges, picnic spots and caves.

The village of Hartington on the southern edge of the Peak District is a gem. Surrounded by dramatic limestone scenery, the village boasts the impressive and imposing St Giles Church, which dates back to AD 1250, an iconic youth hostel, a quintessential village centre and some fine eating and drinking establishments. Thankfully for the wild swimmer the River Dove passes close by, thoughtfully pausing en route to Dove Dale to carve out Pike Pool half way along Beresford Dale. Charles Cotton, who spent much time fishing in the river here, named the pool after the grey monolith or pike (think 'spear') that thrusts out of the water. Cotton was an English poet and writer best known for translating the work of French philosopher Michel de Montaigne, for his contributions to *The Compleat Angler* and for his influential book *The Compleat Gamester*, one of the earliest known directories of English games. He hailed from Beresford and his name is synonymous with the area; one of the hotels in Hartington bears his name.

The walk begins at the Hartington Farm Shop and Café, an impressive establishment close to the pay & display car park. Follow the footpath up steps next to the building, through fields and beyond into Morson Wood, a young woodland planted by the late Les Morson and family in 1994. A pleasant path leads into the woodland to arrive at Beresford Dale and the River Dove. Mornings can be damp and humid, a microclimate common within the confines of the limestone valleys in this part of the Peak District. The stone path is sometimes slick with condensation, the vegetation overhead hanging low and heavy with dew. A quaint footbridge over the river leads to an open area next to an impressively proportioned pool **S1**. At the back of the pool a

INFORMATION

DISTANCE: 5km
TIME: 2–3 hours
MAP: OS Explorer OL24 The Peak District – White Peak Area
PARKING: Pay & display car park in Hartington village (SK 127 602; 53.1391, -1.8114)
PUBLIC TRANSPORT: Moorlands Connect on-demand bus service (Moorlandsconnect.co.uk)
SWIMMING: Pike Pool **S1**, paddling spots downriver by the bridges **S2** + **S3**
PLACES OF INTEREST: Hartington, Pike Pool, caves
REFRESHMENTS: Hartington village has a number of cafés and pubs
VARIANTS: For more pools and limestone grandeur, you can extend your walk on a there-and-back foray down Wolfscote Dale, after direction point **2** + **S3**

large grey limestone pinnacle rises straight from the water, Cotton's 'Pike'. As you swim beneath the rock, its reflection stretched out before you, it feels distinctly prehistoric, like a scene from The Lost World.

Walking downriver from Pikes Pool, you will notice that the river reverts to a quiet brook babbling through solid walls of greenery spotted in summertime with the brilliant pink of the invasive intruder Himalayan balsam before arriving at another bridge and another clearing. This one lies in the shade of a stand of huge trees, next to a beach and shallow dammed-pool **S2**. We cross the narrow wooden bridge into a lovely meadow, wild flowers swaying in the breeze. At the far end of the meadow is a third bridge and yet another shallow

pool **S3**. This is your turnaround point. Don't cross this bridge. Before beginning the walk back, look up the hill towards the limestone cliffs and you will spy a cave mouth. It is well worth a quick foray up the hill to investigate it. With a square entrance, a level floor polished to cathedral quality by the passage of feet over time and sufficient standing room for a dozen, it must surely have been a refuge for countless people over millennia. The view from inside the cave, down towards Wolfscote Dale, would happily grace a guidebook to the area.

The return walk follows a combination of bridleways (actually a National Cycle Route), footpaths and quiet lanes, climbing a fairly steep 70m of ascent before dropping most of the way back down as we descend into Hartington.

1 Park in Parson's Field pay & display car park on the S edge of Hartington village. Walk out of the car park onto the main road (B5054) and turn L. After 50m the Hartington Farm Shop & Café will be on your R. Cross the road and take the public footpath to Dove Dale, up steps along the R side of the building. Public loos on the R. Go through a small metal gate onto a gravel track heading uphill through a field. Follow for 300m to a pair of small wooden gates in two stone walls. Go through both gates to continue across more fields, past wooden posts, to the edge of Morson Wood. (1.1km total) The fields in this section may contain cows.

2 Enter Morson Wood and continue due S to soon arrive at the River Dove. Follow the river for 400m to Beresford Dale and Pike Pool **S1**. The pool lies immediately downriver from a wooden footbridge and is notable for a limestone pillar on its far bank. Continue for a further 300m to another bridge by a copse of shady trees and good paddling/picnicking **S2**. Cross the narrow bridge and turn R to walk along a faint vehicle track through a meadow for 300m to another bridge (which you don't cross), where there is more dipping opportunity **S3**.

3 Before beginning the homeward leg, it is worth heading up the hill to the cave entrances visible from the bridge. Once back at the river, head due N, uphill, on the public bridleway (National Cycle Route 549) until you reach the top of the hill after about 350m. Continue to follow the walled track around to the R, rather than crossing the stile into the field, until you reach Reynards Lane, a very quiet tarmac road.

4 Turn L. Continue for 250m to a very narrow gap in the stone wall on your L and a small wooden gate. Go through the gap and gate to cross the field, exiting through another narrow gap in the wall to join a walled vehicle track. Follow for 600m before rejoining Reynards Lane.

5 Turn L and follow Reynards Lane back into Hartington village. (2km)

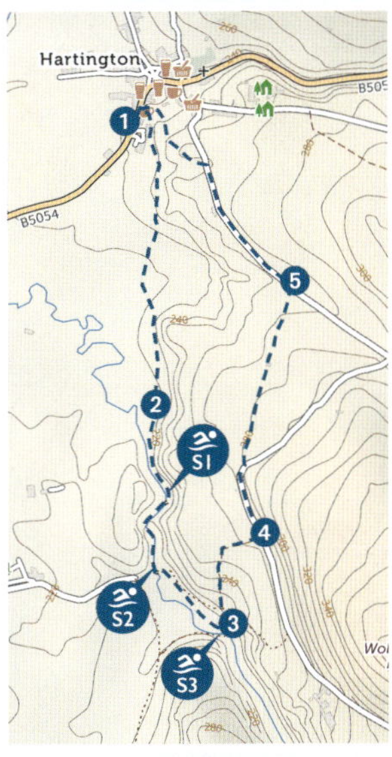

BLAKE MERE & RAMSHAW ROCKS

Swim in the balmy waters of the perfect high moorland Blake Mere pool, and picnic under the imposing skyline of Ramshaw Rocks.

DISTANCE: 8.7km
TIME: 3–4 hours
MAP: OS Explorer OL24 The Peak District – White Peak Area
PARKING: Lay-by on road fork next to Blake Mere (SK 040 612; 53.1485, -1.9409)
PUBLIC TRANSPORT: 108 Bus between Leek and Buxton stops at The Winking Man pub on the A53, approximately 1km from the route, 2.5km from the start/finish. Moorlands Connect on-demand bus service (Moorlandsconnect.co.uk)
SWIMMING: Amazing Blake Mere pool **SI** at the beginning and end of walk
PLACES OF INTEREST: Blake Mere Pool, Ramshaw Rocks
REFRESHMENTS: None
VARIANTS: Ramshaw Rocks offers nearly a kilometre of scrambling and weaselling along its ramparts and buttresses. If you have kids with you or enjoy rock-hopping, you will want to allow additional time to explore and play before heading back

This walk comes with a stern warning: without offline maps on your phone, navigation will be challenging. While the main focus of the outing, Blake Mere Pool, is immediately next to the parking area, the route over to Ramshaw Rocks tackles a very poor bridleway and a section of the Churnet Way that clearly sees little use and which has not only fallen into obscurity but has also been fenced and walled off in one area. The loss of public footpaths is a well-documented phenomenon that any lover of the countryside should be mindful of. We have included this walk in the book to draw attention to this decline. Not only does it link Blake Mere Pool with Ramshaw Rocks, two iconic spots, but it passes through some lovely, little-travelled countryside on 'paths' that could do with some love and attention. Downloading the appropriate offline maps onto your phone before departure should allow you to identify where you are on the sections that are not waymarked and potentially covered in shoulder-high bracken! Whatever, it will be an adventurous outing and one you will remember. Let it be for good reasons!

Part of the route skirts the edge of a Ministry of Defence shooting range, onto which you most definitely do not want to stray. The range is bounded to the west by the A53 Leek to Buxton main road, to the east by Dry Stones and Morridge, to the south by South Swainsmoor and to the north by North Swainsmoor. It is fully enclosed by fencing, and signs state that entry is forbidden because of possible unexploded ordnance. You should be fine tackling this route at any time, as it does not stray into the zone, but we recommend you check the firing times (Gov.uk/government/publications/leek-and-upper-hulme-firing-times). If you see flags flying to your right on your approach to the parking area, this indicates that an exercise is under way.

Warnings out of the way, let's get to the point of why we've included such a problematic route. Blake Mere Pool is an absolute gem **S1**. The size of a small football pitch, it nestles in a natural dip in the moors high, high above Leek. Surrounded by higher ground on all sides, it doesn't catch much wind and, at 1.5–2m deep, the water, black with peat, warms quickly to positively balmy temperatures on a hot summer's day. It is ringed by soft grass and moss, with bright-blue dragonflies darting among beards of white cotton grass. The pool's edge is thick with tadpoles and teeny frogs. It is such a beautiful spot that you will almost certainly want to stop here at the start and at the end of your walk. The water temperature rose four degrees during the four hours of our excursion! Views from the knoll just a few metres above the pool's western edge are spectacular. The jagged black teeth of Ramshaw Rocks lie in the foreground, the Roaches and Hen Cloud just beyond. Far into the west on a clear winter's day it is possible, with a telephoto lens or some binoculars, to see the dockyard cranes of Liverpool and the snowy summit of Yr Wyddfa, Wales's highest peak. It's also a magical spot for a late-evening sunset swim.

Local legend has it that the pool is home to a mermaid. There are other 'mermaid's pools' in the Peak District, including the nearby Doxey Pool atop the Roaches. Two different stories explain the origin of the Blake Mere legend. The more appealing of the two speaks of a mariner who fell in love with a mermaid while in foreign lands. He returned home with her and she lived in the pool so they could be close to each other.

The less wholesome tale tells of a local woman who rejected the romantic advances of a man named Joshua Linnet. He falsely accused her of witchcraft, for which she was sentenced to death by drowning in Blake Mere Pool. As she drowned, she cursed him with her dying breath. Days later his bloodied body was found by the pool. Legend has it that animals will not drink from the pool and birds will not fly over it, as the woman's spirit turned into a mermaid which haunts the pool. It is reputed to be bottomless and connected to Doxey Pool by an underwater tunnel. It is said that locals once tried draining the pool to see if it was bottomless, but the mermaid emerged and threatened to flood Leek and Leekfrith if they did not stop what they were doing! A swim in the pool will reveal that the silty bottom is only a couple of metres from the surface, but there is enough storytelling there to entertain your friends and/or kids for the whole walk – but perhaps don't begin until after your first dip!

The walk begins from the south end of the pool as it takes a cross-country route across open access land to a large wooden stile over a stone wall **2**. Cross the stile and search out a well-used sheep track that contours around the hillside below the road to a building about 700m away. Follow the track, skirting underneath the building to a fence which runs downhill **3**. Other than the stile, there is little to indicate that you are on any sort of right of way; this is the tone for most of the walk. Follow the fence line down the hill, past a gate, to a bridleway, not easily recognised as such. Continue along the bridleway **4** into a narrow valley bottom clogged with trees, occasionally feeling as if one is on a track, more often wondering where it has gone! In the valley bottom is a ford from which the bridleway miraculously

appears, passing through a gate and into a narrow-walled defile reminiscent of parts of France. The route then passes to the right of the obvious landmark of a cute 'doer-upper' barn **5**, with many open windows, before arriving at a couple of very unkempt working farms, complete with dogs, cows, sheep, chickens and goats wandering around, with little sign of human occupation, reminiscent of Orwell's Animal Farm **6**.

Beyond the farms things get really interesting! The route joins the Churnet Way **7**, a 50km long-distance footpath that starts in the Staffordshire Moorlands and finishes near Rocester, where it joins the River Dove. Sadly, this section of the footpath, which climbs out of the valley bottom to Ramshaw Rocks above, sees very little use and, some time ago, a fence, a wall and some farming machinery were placed in its way! Offline maps on your phone will show you exactly where the path is; otherwise, you are aiming for the imposing bastions of Ramshaw Rocks, which lie just above the A53. Occasional rotting fingerpost signs and a broken fence post blocking the path indicate that there was indeed once a path here, but you would be forgiven for going off piste. The path

arrives at the very busy (and very fast) stretch of the A53 directly opposite a minor paved road, just a hundred metres below the edge of the rocks **8**.

Weaselling through the boulders, pinnacles and spires will bring out your younger self! Picnicking is advised. Once rested it should be a relatively simple task to reverse your route from here as far as the fords at the bottom of the valley **9**, the point at which you joined the Churnet Way. Now more complex route finding is called for to trace your way up the opposite side of the valley back to the approach road to Blake Mere Pool. The path passes old gates and a stile, decaying fingerposts, sections of boardwalk, all the while following the edge of the MoD firing range **10**. Halfway up the hill it is well worth stopping for a break at a lovely copse of trees, some of which are hollowed out. Low-rise military buildings dot the landscape to your left, presumably foxholes and vantage points for exercising soldiers. While the route finding is tricky, and the terrain challenging, the situation feels remote and very wild.

Once you arrive at the tarmac road, turn right and follow it for 1.6km **11** back to the car, and a well-deserved second dip in Blake Mere Pool.

1 Park in the lay-by at the fork in the road next to Blake Mere. Cross the road and follow the track for a few metres before dropping down to the pool itself for a swim before you start **S1**.

2 Walk along to the far S-edge of the pool and follow indistinct and discontinuous paths in the bilberry for 300m to a large wooden stile over a wall. Cross the stile and continue, bearing L, to follow a sheep path below the road which contours (stays level) around the hillside for a further 700m to a building with a large glass floor-to-ceiling window overlooking the valley. Follow the fenced border of the building on the R side to a fence which runs down into the valley.

3 At the fence turn R to follow it downhill for 500m to the second wooden gate. Don't go through the gate. On the other side of the gate is a blue-painted sign asking walkers to keep to the bridleway on the R.

4 From the gate continue in roughly the same direction on a very poorly marked 'bridleway', down to the tree-filled bottom of the valley 300m below. You will pass close to a distinctive electricity pylon with overhead cables splitting in three directions. The bridleway winds its way through a confluence of small streams which meet under the trees. Cross the confluence on stepping stones and then climb back out up a more obvious track,

going through a seven-bar metal gate, to come out into open fields. (400m total)

5 Walk towards a distinctive old barn with six window apertures, passing it on the R. Continue through another (six-bar) metal gate next to a telegraph pole. Head through the meadow to a farm. Don't take the direct path through the farm gate; a short way uphill is another metal gate (seven-bar) which is actually on the bridleway. Pass through this to then approach the farm directly. Enter the farmyard through two old metal gates that lean against one another. Turn R to walk between farm buildings, among farm animals. Be assured, you are on a permissive path.

6 Leave the farm through yet another metal gate on a track past a small barn on your R. At 200m from the farm is another farm. Follow the track through this farm too (be aware of cows). On the edge of the farm the track goes both L and R. Leave the track here and continue in the same direction, N, for 200m across a field (more cows). At the boundary of the field the track goes through a wooden six-bar gate and fords a very small stream before snaking through trees and fording another stream.

7 You are now on the Churnet Way, contrary to appearances. Follow the seldom-used and not-at-all obvious path fairly steeply uphill through the field to the NW, and then W, arriving at a fence on

the edge of a coniferous plantation. A broken fence post indicates the place where the 'path' crosses into the trees. Continue in the same direction, through the trees, over a broken wall on the upper edge of the plantation, into a field of long grass, past a fenced-off well (there is an old Churnet Way plaque on one of the fence posts) and old farm machinery, to a wooden stile on the roadside of the very busy A53. Cross the road with care and follow the minor road on the opposite side for 100m to a footpath on the R leading to Ramshaw Rocks and Edge.

8 Explore as much of the Edge as you like before retracing your steps all the way back to the beginning of Point 7.

9 After crossing the westernmost stream described in **6**, head NE on the public footpath (the Churnet Way). Initially, this track is well-marked, but as it bends L (N), break R to drop into a wooded stream bed. Cross the stream next to a fence which bridges the banks, climbing the far bank on old tree roots. At 100m from the trees/bank there is a distinctive wooden fence and stile at a confluence of three broken stone walls (difficult to find as the path is not obvious). Cross the stile. After 300m there is an attractive copse of about five trees, with a section of wooden fence visible bottom L. Head towards this, avoiding the boggy trough on the L. Next to the copse, spanning the boggy trough, is a dilapidated wooden walkway.

10 Continue past the copse in the same direction for 500m, following occasional signs of a footpath, doglegging L and back R halfway along this section, through a small wooden gate. MoD signs on the L mark the boundary of the firing range. At 500m from the copse, turn 90 degrees L and continue for a further 500m. Follow faint paths, old fingerposts and a few wooden dilapidated boardwalks skirting the edge of the firing range to eventually arrive at an access track. (1.3km of challenging and often bewildering route-finding!)

11 Turn R on the track, follow it for 400m to the road. Turn R and follow the road for 1.6km back to the car and pool (keeping R at the fork after 200m).

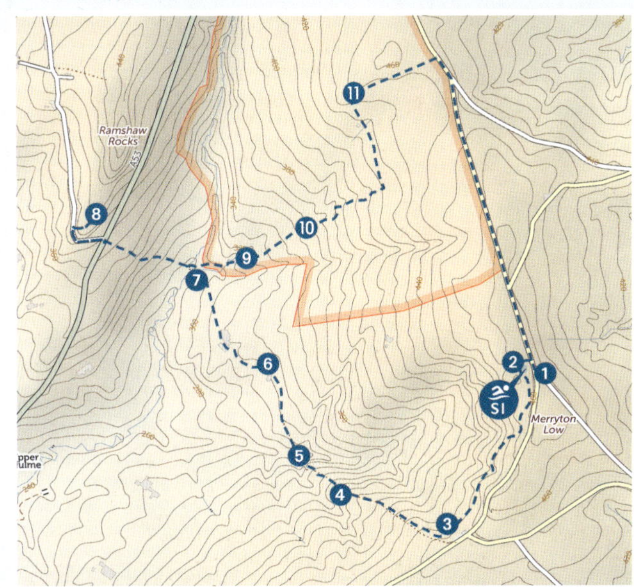

THREE SHIRES HEAD

Where three counties and two rivers meet lies Panniers Pool, but upstream away from the crowds are a host of quieter pools and waterfalls to rival any others in the national park.

Three Shires Head is a great example of why a book like this deserves a place on your bookshelf. When we first moved to the Peak District many years ago and started asking about good places to swim, Three Shires Head came up again and again. It's a grand name, a confluence of two rivers at the point where three counties meet. It has an important air about it, surely a swim spot that any self-respecting wild swimmer should visit. For one reason or another we failed to make it there for some time, so the expectation of what it would be like grew. When we finally found our way there, following the basic directions from a guidebook with the quickest route to the pools, it was a chilly and overcast day and our approach was scrappy and disappointing. It was hugely underwhelming and we never went back. Ten years have since rolled by, and it's been necessary to do some proper research for this book; we didn't want you repeating our experience! Suzie Wheway of Peak Swims, a local outdoor swim instructor, not only suggested this lovely route, but has even written it up. Having been stung on our previous ill-researched visit, we felt it necessary to check out Suzie's route choice and instructions and, frankly, we can't fault them! It's a brilliant route, packing in a multitude of pools, most of which you will have to yourselves. If you'd like to experience guided swim-walks of this ilk, then contact Suzie at Peakswims.co.uk

Three Shires Head forms the meeting point of the three counties of Derbyshire, Cheshire and Staffordshire. The River Dane, which runs through it, rises only 3km upstream on Axe Edge Moor. The proximity to its source and elevation at 350m

INFORMATION

DISTANCE: 5km
TIME: 2–3 hours
MAP: OS Explorer OL24 The Peak District – White Peak Area
PARKING: A medium-sized lay-by on the A54 (SK 007 698; 53.2256, -1.9900)
PUBLIC TRANSPORT: 58 bus between Buxton and Macclesfield passes very close to the start of the walk
SWIMMING: Lots of waterfalls with shallow pools **S1** + **S2** in the stream above the main pools at Three Shires Head **S3** and a hidden pool in Reeve Edge Quarry **S4**
PLACES OF INTEREST: Reeve Edge Quarry, Three Shires Head, Danebower Colliery ventilation chimney
REFRESHMENTS: None
VARIANTS: While most folk congregate around the main pools by the bridge, there's a cracker downstream worth seeking out **S5**

mean the water here stays cool all year, so it's the perfect spot for a little burst of cold when lowland waters lose their zing in the height of summer or an opportunity for early acclimatisation in autumn for the winter ahead. While it can get busy on a hot day, this walk takes you via a lesser-trodden path past hidden pools that few explore. If you're looking for peace and tranquillity, heading out early or planning your walk for a cloudy day could mean that you could get the place to yourself.

The walk starts and finishes past the Danebower Colliery chimney **1**. The square, stone-built chimney dates back to the early 1800s, when an extensive coal industry existed around the remote moorland between Macclesfield, Leek and Buxton. Before the miners started work underground each morning, a fire would be lit at the base of the long flue up the hillside to the chimney; the ensuing updraught, known as the Venturi effect, would literally vacuum the stale air out of the mine shaft and tunnels, providing underground ventilation for the miners. This technique was a widely used procedure before the development of industrial mechanical fans. The mine was abandoned in 1922, but the chimney remains today as a listed ancient monument.

As we descend the valley from the chimney, our first swim spot is seen down to the left **S1**, a shallow but perfectly formed jacuzzi plunge pool beneath a small waterfall in the River Dane. Returning to the path, we continue to follow it as it threads its way downhill **2** close to the stream, with numerous opportunities to get in the water **S2** to your left. As the valley sides close in, trees shade the water, giving privacy to the lesser-visited pools up-river from the popular Panniers Pool Bridge (possibly so-called as passing ponies would have stopped here to drink). Here the River

Dane merges with an unnamed stream to form a chaos of pools **S3** and waterfalls, very popular with swimmers. By all means join the fray but explore just upstream and downstream and you will likely find equally good pools and have them all to yourselves.

The return leg is the perfect warm-up to shake off any chills from your moorland plunge **3**. Steel yourself as there is a fair climb ahead before you arrive at Reeve Edge Quarry, developed for the production of gritstone roofing flags, many of which can be seen on local buildings. A large amount of waste was produced in the process of making the flags, as evidenced by the extensive spoil heaps. In among these spoil heaps you may be grateful to discover one last swim spot, a large, shallow pool hemmed in by steep banks of angular stones, which makes access tricky but certainly worthwhile. A waterfall at the pool's lower end means you can even shower before heading home! From here cross the stream above the pool and turn left to return through more spoil heaps to your vehicle.

Thanks, Suzie, for the encouragement and the words!

1 The starting point is a decent-sized lay-by on the A54, overlooking the abandoned Reeve Edge Quarries and the distinctive stone-built chimney of Danebower Colliery. From the lay-by, walk uphill on a narrow path below the level of the road, keeping the chimney to your R, and pass through a large metal farm gate onto a well-used track. After about 100m take a sharp R-hand turn, switching from a stone track to a narrow, grassy footpath. This cuts across and gently down the hillside below the lay-by, and you will pass the chimney again uphill to your R. If you are taking your furry friend along, please note that there are restrictions in place to protect moorland habitats. Dogs must stay on public rights of way and stay on a lead at all times.

2 Continue down the valley. The stream to your L will gradually widen and begin to gently tumble. Look out for pools along this stretch **S1** + **S2**; many are suitable for dipping, with grassy banks on each side. After about 2km you will reach an iconic high-arched packhorse bridge close to a decent selection of pools **S3**. (1.6km)

3 From the bridge take the path through a large metal gate to ascend a narrow valley with a stream to your R. At the next junction take the L-hand fork, still keeping the stream to your R, and then bear L onto a tarmacked road towards Blackclough Farm. Go past the farm, through a wooden farm gate, and bear R, diagonally, across two fields, through a crumbling but well-defined stone wall, to a large gate through a dry-stone wall. Turn L here onto a well-maintained stone track.

4 At the edge of the quarry bear L at the first large rubble pile and follow a well-trodden path through the quarry. This

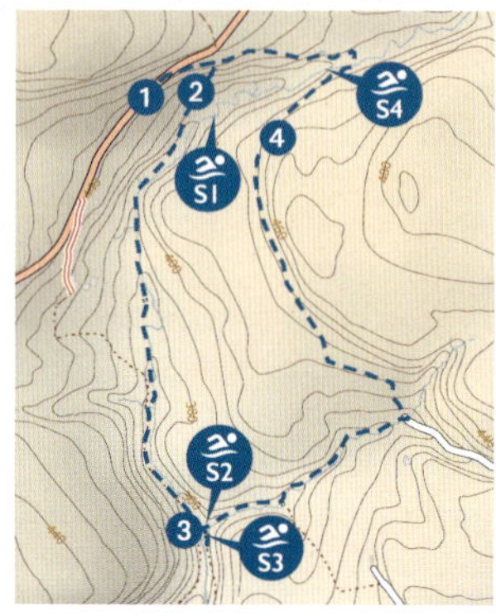

landscape is wholly man-made but is being beautifully reclaimed by nature as bilberry and heather colonise these rocky mounds. Just before the stream crossing is a pool down on your L, which is worth a dip after the climb back up the valley **S4**. Cross the stream via stepping stones and ascend to a small sheepfold. Follow the path to the L, through heather-clad mounds, and retrace your earlier steps back to the start point.

PACKHORSE BRIDGE
& THE GOYT VALLEY

The Goyt Valley is a hidden gem on the edge of the national park. This circular walk explores the wilder upper reaches of the River Goyt before rounding one of the two reservoirs in its lower reaches.

Built in the early-to-mid-1900s to supply the growing town of Stockport with drinking water, Fernilee and Errwood reservoirs remain important today. Although there is vehicular access to the valley, there is no main road so it has retained some of the wild nature it had before the construction began.

The walk begins high on the moors at a small car park next to a teeny reservoir ❶. It is possible to swim in here **S1**; there is even a small beach on the adjacent shore to the car park, but it's fairly shallow and doesn't feel too welcoming with its rocky border. Unlike many walks, this one starts off downhill. It follows a delightful footpath off the moors into a quiet side valley off the Goyt itself. In summer it's thick with shoulder-high bracken, a profusion of wild flowers and birds. At the bottom of the valley is a rather elaborate metal and wooden bridge ❷, suitable for driving a 4x4 or a quad bike over, testimony to the level of farming activity in the area.

Crossing the bridge, we now follow a 4x4 track on a fairly level contour along the valley side, winding towards the reservoir through a couple of old wooden gates. The reservoirs are hidden from view, giving the area an aura of remoteness, and there's no traffic noise and virtually no people. As the track rounds a shoulder ❸, and the reservoir comes into view, it skirts heather-clad moorland which explodes into purple bloom in August.

The prettiest section of the walk comes next: a stunted birch forest ❹ carpeted in lush grasses. This can be a damp area after rain, but much of the bog is avoided by a discontinuous series of

INFORMATION

DISTANCE: 8km
TIME: 2–3 hours
MAP: OS Explorer OL24 The Peak District – White Peak Area
PARKING: Goyt Valley car park: a small unpaved parking area big enough for about 20 vehicles next to a small reservoir high on the moors (SK 024 751; 53.2737, -1.9653)
PUBLIC TRANSPORT: None. The start is just over 3km from Buxton, along Long Hill (A5004)
SWIMMING: Small reservoir by car park **S1**; shallow pools for dipping in the River Goyt, below the packhorse bridge **S2** + **S3**; it is also possible to swim in Errwood Reservoir despite the usual 'No Swimming' signs **S4**
PLACES OF INTEREST: Packhorse bridge, ice cream van at Errwood Reservoir
REFRESHMENTS: Ice cream van at Errwood Reservoir
VARIANTS: More pools can be found upstream of the packhorse bridge. There is an interesting clockwise extension loop around Errwood Hall and Shining Tor if you have the time

wooden walkways. Although it feels less wild as a result, there's a good nature-trail feel to the path as it wends its way towards the main attraction.

Sat about a hundred metres above the River Goyt is a wooden signpost **5** that points down to the packhorse bridge **6**. The stone bridge is really pretty; the sort of pretty that tourists, both from this country and overseas consider as quintessentially British. There are lovely picnic spots immediately by the bridge, but most of the pools are not deep enough for swimming. You now have two options: the easiest route is to follow the footpath and road down the opposite side of the river, back towards the reservoir. However, the adventurous can opt for a delightful few hundred metres of exploration and follow the river itself, most likely getting wet feet in the process. Tucked out of sight, there are small pools deep enough to take a dip **S2** + **S3**. In our opinion the best of these is downstream from a huge fallen tree that spans the river and provides a brilliant climbing frame for youngsters, or adults who are still kids at heart. If you chose the easier waymarked route, the fallen tree is just a little way downstream from where the path drops back down to the river. The best of the pools is 50m downstream from the tree.

Continuing from the pools, the official path remains fairly level as the river drops away, leaving us high above the water, glimpsing reflections and glints of secret pools down below. It's strictly for the adventurous if you want to venture down there!

Finally, the path descends to a car park for Errwood Hall **7**. If you have time and fancy a little more mileage, a thoroughly enjoyable extra loop can be made around Errwood Hall and Shining Tor. On hot days an ice cream van can usually be found in the car park **8**. A little further on is Errwood Reservoir. Frustratingly, despite the fact

that it has a sailing and kayaking club, swimming is discouraged by an ugly plethora of scaremongering signage, quite out of keeping in this lovely area. There is evidence that plenty of people swim though, with lots of picnic spots on the grassy banks **S4**. Jumping from the bridge has obviously been commonplace in the past, as there is now a prison-grade fence to prevent this. So sad.

The walk continues by the side of the reservoir. Although it is a paved road, even on a hot summer's weekend all is peaceful and there is little traffic in this neck of the woods, and the pleasant footpath still manages to find ways to avoid the tarmac. As you leave the reservoir for the long climb back to your vehicle, **9** there's a path that runs parallel to the road **10**, steeply gaining a beautiful grassy shoulder. The small reservoir at the car park may well be a lot more appealing than it was at the start of the walk **S1**.

1 As you leave the car park in a SW direction there is a small reservoir in which it is possible to swim **S1**. Ignore the tarmac road and the parallel track to the L. Head downhill on a path L of the track. Follow this for 700m, losing about 75m, to a junction just before Wildmoorstone Brook.

2 Cross the brook on a metal and wooden bridge in a S direction. Follow a wide 4x4 track which curves to the R, passing through two wooden gates, and then back L. (700m)

3 Strike off the 4x4 track to the R at a wooden signpost. Follow a narrow footpath towards stone walls and bracken. The path follows a stone wall to the R before opening out onto the grass and heather of an open hillside and then heading into a wood of stunted birch. (1km)

4 Continue on wooden duckboards through the pretty trees until another wooden signpost. (700m)

5 Turn R to drop down to the River Goyt and the packhorse bridge. (100m)

6 Cross the bridge and turn R along a paved road for 300m, then take a footpath down towards the river on the R, to shallow pools for dipping and cooling off **S2** + **S3**. Now follow the footpath through the deciduous woods for a further kilometre. Keep L on the footpath/track when it joins the paved road. (1.3km)

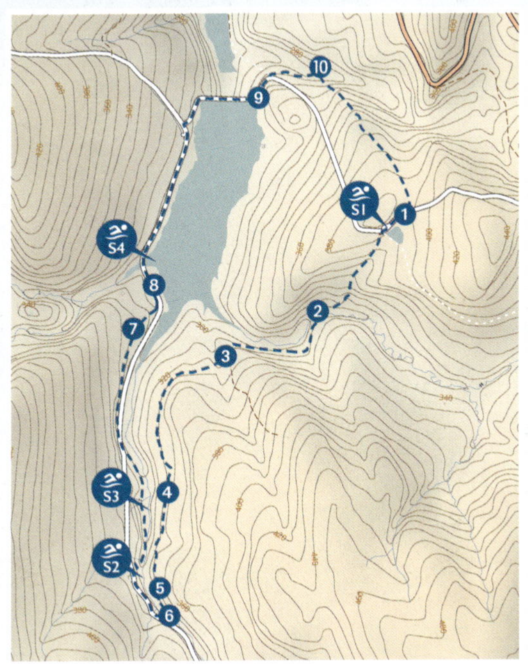

7 At a crossroads with stone gateposts and a metal gate, turn R to drop steeply down to Errwood Hall car park by Errwood Reservoir (ice cream van on hot days) **S4**.

8 Follow the paved road and parallel footpath (on the L of the road) along and then around the end of Errwood Reservoir for 1.6km.

9 At the T-junction on the E side of the dam turn L and continue for about 100m to a footpath, passing through a wooden fence on the L into the woods.

10 Follow a path through the woods for 200m to a small wooden bridge over a trickling brook. There is a confluence of wooden fences and a gate here. Before crossing the bridge, take the faint path on the R, and then continue on the path, heading SE, as it climbs along the edge of the woods before opening out onto a grassy shoulder. Continue for 800m, climbing 100m in the process to arrive back at the car park.